Stars, Cars & Infamy
Martin Buckley

CONTENTS

MOTORBOOKS INTERNATIONAL

First published in 2003 by Motorbooks International, an imprint of MBI Publishing Company, Galtier Plaza, Suite 200, 380 Jackson Street, St. Paul, MN 55101-3885 USA

Motorbooks International titles are also available at discounts in bulk quantity for industrial or sales-promotional use. For details write to Special Sales Manager at Motorbooks International Wholesalers & Distributors, Galtier Plaza, Suite 200, 380 Jackson Street, St. Paul, MN 55101-3885 USA.

Talk to the publisher about this book:
rob@motorbooksinternational.co.uk

ISBN 0-7603-1687-2

Printed in China

Introduction

Martin Buckley's book is a truly original concept, a brilliant exploration of the symbiotic rela-tionships between the stars and their cars. It's all in here, the good, the bad and the ugly, reeking with anecdotes that encompass comedy, tragedy and the psychology of the owners, from the flamboyant to the *cogniscenti*. Compelling personalities, legends of their Zeitgeist one and all. This is an invaluable encyclopaedia of knowledge for anyone interested in four wheels, two reels or icons of a bi-gone era. A must for all car enthusiasts and film buffs alike. Flicking through this book was like a drive down Memory Lane for me when I was a reluctant 'star' touring around in my Aston Martin. I could almost smell the Castrol GTX, Havana cigars and Chanel No.5 on every page. Take an Oscar and the chequered flag Martin, this book is a winner.

Bruce Reynolds, Great Train Robber and author of *Crossing the Line: Autobiography of a Thief*

1 CELEBRITY CARS, CRASHES AND NEAR MISSES

Car accidents involving the great, the good and the notorious seem to attract two classes of raisin-brained fruitcake – the conspiracy theorist and the voyeur. The former has spent years compiling a thesis that proves, without doubt, that the deaths of James Dean, Albert Camus, Eddie Cochran and many others were the product of an international cartel of evil, comprising the KGB, the CIA, MI6, Mossad, Deuxième Bureau, Captain Black of the Mysterons and Mr. Meeker from Rentaghost.

Details such as the victim not wearing a seatbelt or being driven too fast by a very inexperienced driver are ignored in favour of arguments scientifically proved by watching every episode of the *X Files* 25 times.

Then there is the voyeur, the breed of motoring enthusiast for whom bad TV compilations of road accidents were marketed. Usually, their fascination dates from an early age, the sound of an ambulance bell having a Pavlovian response in their youthful minds. Forty years later you may see them gently salivating over tabloid pictures of motorway pile-ups. You occasionally see them on a motorway hard shoulder with a video camera to record pile-ups of note: any link between such behaviour and banger racing remains entirely unproven.

KEITH RICHARDS:
Turned down reunion with Lena

Keith Richards, who formed the Rolling Stones with childhood friend Mick Jagger in 1962, bought a new Bentley Continental Flying Spur four years later as one of the first major spoils of their success. At £8,000 it cost him almost half as much as Redlands, his moated country house in Sussex in the south of England. The 23-year-old was inspired to buy the car because of the Bentley's literary connections with James Bond. He named it Blue Lena after singer Lena Horne and fitted it with a record player, dark windows and Turkish embassy flags to keep the law guessing. He loved the car and kept it for 10 years. The final parting came in 1976 when Keef, returning tired and emotional after a concert, fell asleep at the wheel. Lena crashed through a barrier and left the road. Richards was uninjured but was forced to spend the night in a police cell. In 1996 the car came up for auction but Mr Richards didn't seem interested in a reunion with Lena – assuming that he could remember her, that is.

Blue Lena, post-accident, sometime in the '90s, outside the house of a new owner.
Pic: Martin Buckley Archive.

"The final parting came in 1976 when Keef, tired and emotional after a concert at Stafford, fell asleep at the wheel. Lena crashed through a barrier and left the road."

The Daily Mirror picture shows the mangled Consul driven by taxi driver George Martin who lost his way while driving Cochran to London and crashed, killing the rock star.
Pic: Historic Newspapers

EDDIE COCHRAN:
Tragedy only hours before flight home

The town of Chippenham, Wiltshire, still has a sad resonance for ageing rockers for it was there, on April 17, 1960, that American rock singer Eddie Cochran died at the end of a triumphant tour of Britain. The MkII Ford Consul taxi taking Eddie, fellow rocker Gene Vincent and friends from Bristol to London left 50-yard skidmarks on a dry road surface before hitting a street lamp, badly damaging the rear seat area. The rock stars were looking forward to flying home the following day as taxi driver George Martin gunned the Consul through Bath towards the outskirts of Chippenham on the A4, long before the building of the M4 motorway. It was late at night and Martin took a wrong turn; while rushing to pick up the route again, he lost control of the Consul. He was uninjured and later convicted of causing the death of Edward Ray Cochran, aged 21, by driving a motor vehicle at a dangerous speed. He was fined £50 and disqualified from driving for 15 years. Elderly Teddy boys and younger fans of the singer-songwriter still leave commemorations at the spot where the Consul crashed. One of the police officers on the scene of the accident was police cadet David Dee (later of the band Dave Dee, Dozy, Beaky, Mick and Tich).

> "There were 50-yard long skidmarks on the road and evidence of the car colliding heavily with a street lamp before it came to rest against the kerb..."

Daily Mirror

MON APR. 18 1960

2½

No. 17,522

'ROCK' STAR DIES IN CRASH

● PICTURED ABOVE. Singer Eddie Cochran. LEFT: The wreckage of the car after the crash which killed him.

By NED GRANT

AMERICAN rock 'n' roll singing star Eddie Cochran, 21, died yesterday after a car taking him to London Airport crashed.

Among the three other passengers in the car when it crashed at Chippenham, Wilts, on Saturday night were two Americans—"rock" singer Gene Vincent, 25, and girl song writer Sharon Sheeley, 20.

Last night Miss Sheeley

going steady since they met two years ago.

"Eddie was the first and only boy friend Sharon ever had. They were terribly in love, and were planning to marry. They were unofficially engaged."

The car's driver, George Martin, of Hartcliffe, Bristol, was unhurt.

Cochran—with Sharon, Gene Vincent and the fourth passenger, Camberwell theatrical agent Patrick Thomkins, 29—was taken to hospital.

America-bound

Just after four o'clock yesterday afternoon, Cochran died

The toll: 33 dead
632 injured so far

Champion pour la cinquième fois le père tranquille du volant a éclipsé une fois encore les "comingmen" anglais. Il a relevé pour l'an prochain le défi des Américains à Indianopolis.

Ce touriste au poignet luxé, devant sa Lancia endommagée, est l'as Manuel Fangio. A 160 à l'heure, il a évité sur la route de Fidenza un accident mortel. Photo Giancolombo.

Fangio looks slightly sheepish after his autostrada drama.
Pic: Jack Romano

JUAN-MANUEL FANGIO:
Truck driver thought he'd killed 'The King'

Even the greatest drivers make errors of judgement on the road. In the mid-1950s, Juan-Manuel Fangio, who had just been crowned world motor racing champion for the fifth time, was driving his Lancia Aurelia B20 along an Italian freeway at more than 100mph. He was showing off a little to his two passengers when a truck suddenly pulled out of the other lane, misjudging Fangio's speed. The champion put the Lancia into a massive slide to get rid of some speed, went around the lorry and nearly got away with it, but just clipped a marker post and sent it flying, damaging the side of the car slightly. It was a superb manoeuvre, worthy of 'The King'. Fangio injured a wrist but his passengers were unharmed, though a little shaken. The next person along was the lorry driver, unamused by the incident and unaware of who was driving. He approached the Lancia, to see Fangio slumped over the wheel and became deeply upset, thinking he'd killed the world champion. In the end everyone was OK and the Lancia was taken to Maserati's works and fixed (Fangio was contracted to the manufacturer at the time).

"Suddenly a lorry pulled out of the other lane, and Fangio put the Lancia into a massive slide."

JAYNE MANSFIELD:
Unglamorous death for busty actress

Jayne Mansfield, born Vera Jayne Palmer, was a glamorous actress best remembered for her bust (publicised as 40" to 46" at various times, with a waist sometimes measured at 18"). Death came in a most unglamorous way: she was a passenger in a 1966 Buick Electra that slammed into the back of an insecticide truck on a winding, narrow two-lane highway at 2.25am on June 28, 1967. Mansfield, aged 34, had finished a show at a club in Biloxi, Mississippi, and was heading for a television appearance in New Orleans the following day. Her companion – attorney Sam Brody, 40 – and driver Ronnie Harrison, 20, were also killed. The impact sheared off the top of the car and Mansfield died of severe head injuries but was not decapitated, as was luridly reported at the time. Mansfield's three children, lying asleep on the back seat, escaped almost unscathed. In April 1998, the Tragedy in US History Museum in St. Augustine, Florida, closed and offered for auction its entire collection, which included Mansfield's 1966 Buick Electra. It failed to find a buyer.

"The impact sheared the top of the car off but the kids emerged relatively unscathed, because they were asleep in the back."

For glamorous Jayne Mansfield, adopting a typically provocative pose, death came in a smash with an insecticide truck.
Pic: Pictorial Press

The Playboy Prince gets into his Mercedes Gullwing
after a hard day spent squandering his vast wealth.

Pic: Pictorial Press

ALY KHAN:
Last drive in a Lancia for Playboy Prince

The Aga Khan III complained his playboy offspring cared only for 'fast horses, fast cars and fast women.' True to form, Prince Aly Khan met his death driving a fast car to a lavish high society dinner on the French Riviera in the company of a beautiful woman.

Aly Khan was one of the original 1950s jet-setters, living a hedonistic playboy lifestyle on the Riviera. He had been famously married to Rita Hayworth and had well-publicised affairs with a string of other actresses and models: Kim Novak, Gene Tierney and Juliet Greco were all associated with him. On May 12, 1960, his friend Lorraine Bonnet was hosting dinner on her estate in Ville d'Avray. Among the invited guests were André Malraux, Baron and Baroness Guy de Rothschild, Stavros Niarchos, Porfirio Rubirosa (who would famously kill himself in a Ferrari), Mr and Mrs Arturo Lopez-Willshaw, Princess Polignac – and Prince Aly Khan with the model Bettina. Driving his brand new Lancia Flaminia GT on a steep road in Suresnes, Aly Khan hit a Simca Aronde coming the other way as he tried to overtake. He was taken immediately to a hospital at St. Cloud but died of his injuries.

"Driving his brand new Lancia Flaminia GT on a steep road on the French Riviera, Aly Khan hit a Simca Aronde coming the other way as he tried to overtake."

MONTGOMERY CLIFT:
Chevy smash wrecked heart-throb's career

"Clift was found slumped under the steering wheel with his face hideously lacerated, his jaw broken and choking on his two front teeth which had been knocked down his throat"

Montgomery Clift was a sensitive young movie heart-throb and a major influence on Marlon Brando and James Dean. By the age of 35, he was thrice Oscar-nominated and one of the most sought-after talents in Hollywood, who could count Elizabeth Taylor among his best friends. In 1956 he and Taylor began filming *Raintree County* and it was when he was returning from a dinner party at his co-star's house, driving down a steep twisty descent towards Sunset Boulevard, that he lost control of his Chevrolet on a dangerous curve and hit a telegraph pole. Clift was found slumped under the steering wheel with his face badly lacerated, his jaw broken and choking on two front teeth which had been knocked down his throat: Elizabeth Taylor saved his life by pulling them out. The doctors did what they could with his battered features but the left side of his face was frozen. Already unstable and moody, his career and his health went into decline in an avalanche of pills and booze and he made only a handful of films before his death in 1966.

Monty makes sure they shoot his good side. The car is a DeSoto.
Pic: Pictorial Press

ROWAN PILES HIS £650k McLAREN INTO £600 METRO

WRECKED: Badly dented bonnet of Atkinson's fabulous F1 McLaren after yesterday's accident

FORTUNATE: The £600 Metro escaped virtually unmarked, suffering only a bent number plate

Embarrassed Mr Bean stays mum

ROWAN ATKINSON:
A real-life Mr Bean behind the wheel

Rowan Atkinson is famously publicity shy so it's not difficult to imagine what a plonker he felt when he crashed his £650,000 McLaren F1 – bought to celebrate the success of his *Mr Bean* movie – into the back of a Mini Metro in 1999. The front of the 230mph McLaren supercar was wrecked but the driver of the Metro, Margaret Greenhalgh, suffered only minor whiplash injuries in the accident on the A6 at Forton in the north of England. The star, also famous for his role as Blackadder in the eponymous TV series, reportedly asked police not to name him.

Atkinson walked away unhurt from another pile-up when his Aston Martin Zagato hit a barrier during a race at the Croft race circuit, County Durham, in the north of England in 2001. Atkinson does better when airborne: he took the controls of a light aircraft while on holiday in the same year in Africa when the pilot passed out.

Rowan Atkinson reportedly hates publicity, so once again here's that picture of his crashed 230mph, £650,000 supercar.
Pic: Historic Newspapers

"The star, also famous for his role as Blackadder in the eponymous TV series, reportedly asked police not to name him following the accident in the 230mph supercar."

DIRK BOGARDE:
Haunted by wartime killing

In 1945, a young subaltern lost control of his Jeep in the Indian monsoon rains. He cannoned into a column of army deserters, killing two of them instantly. Captain Derek van den Bogaerde was completely exonerated but the trauma of the accident always remained with him. He made his screen debut in 1948 and, as heart-throb Dirk Bogarde, often portrayed war heroes, in *They who dare*, *The sea shall not have them*, *Ill met by moonlight* and other films. He became a wealthy man, living in the south of France, and owned a succession of Silver Clouds, but he never drove again.

"He cannoned into two soldiers, who were a part of a column of army deserters and killed both of them instantly."

In the 1961 movie *Victim*, Dirk Bogarde was seen
in a Bristol 406, fitting transport for a barrister.
Pic: Pictorial Press

X100 presidential limousine with a
choice of optional head protection.
Pic: Ford Motor Company

JOHN F KENNEDY:
Died in the Lincoln that toured with him

This Lincoln Continental X100, specially modified by coachbuilders Hess and Eisenhardt, toured the world with President John F Kennedy. It was the car in which he was shot in Dallas, Texas, in 1963 and became a major piece of evidence in the Warren Commission's investigation. Its cracked windscreen still sits in the American National Archives but the car was put back into service after a complete refit including extensive bullet-proofing that added a ton to its weight. Presidents Johnson, Nixon and Ford used the car until it was finally taken out of service and returned to its owners, Ford, in 1977 (the White House rented it for $500 a year). The Lincoln is living out its retirement in the Henry Ford Museum in Dearborn, Michigan.

"The car was put back into service after a complete refit which included extensive bullet-proofing that added a ton to its weight."

MARC BOLAN:
Probably Mini's most famous victim

Alec Issigonis, inspiration behind the 1959 Mini, had little interest in passive safety which is why it was never first choice for an accident. Glam rocker Marc Bolan was probably the car's most famous victim. In the early hours of September 16, 1977, he was in his Mini 1275GT, driven by his girlfriend Gloria 'Tainted Love' Jones along Queens Ride at the southern edge of Barnes Common, south west London. The Mini left the road as it crossed a bridge, shot through a fence and smashed into a sycamore tree. Bolan's side took the brunt of the blow: he was thrown into the back of the car and killed instantly. To this day Bolan fans hold a vigil at that inoffensive sycamore tree on the anniversary of the accident.

"Bolan's side took the brunt of the blow; he was thrown into the back of the car and killed instantly."

Marc, Glor

Bolan death shocks the pop world

toddler son Rolan.

By KEVIN O'LONE

THE pop world was last night mourning the death of superstar Marc Bolan.

Tributes flooded in for the 30-year-old singer who was killed in a car smash early yesterday.

Rock star David Bowie almost collapsed when he heard the news at his home in Switzerland.

And Radio One D J Tony Blackburn described Bolan's death as a "terrible tragedy."

The London-born pop star, who fought his way back from drug addiction and alcoholism, died when a purple Mini driven by his girlfriend, American singer Gloria Jones, crashed into a tree.

Thirty-year-old Gloria, the mother of Bolan's 20-month-old son Rolan, was recovering last night from a fractured jaw and severe face cuts.

The couple were returning from a night out at a West End restaurant when their car smashed into a tree on a narrow bend at Barnes Common, London.

Steve Harley, singer with Cockney Rebel, who was Bolan's closest friend in the rock business, said from Los Angeles last night:

"He was a star in the truest sense and I'll miss him more than I can say."

Singer Helen Shapiro, 30, who was at school with Bolan in London's East End, said: "Marc was always a rebel, even when he was nine.

Comeback

"We used to sing Elvis Presley songs at the time, and had a lot of fun.

"His death is a terrible shock."

Ironically, Bolan—the son of a Jewish cosmetics sales-man—died as he was ma[ ] a comeback.

Bolan and his b[ ] T-Rex, were re-establish[ ] themselves with a hig[ ] successful children's televi[ ] show on ITV.

Four of the six pre-reco[ ] shows called Marc [ ] already been shown an[ ] was decided yesterday [ ] Bolan's parents to go al[ ] and show the remaining [ ] programmes.

Last night, Gloria had [ ] not been told of Bo[ ] death.

Mr. Tony Howard, man[ ] for both of them, s[ ] "Gloria is in a state of [ ] shock."

Bolan's violent end in the 1275GT only made page three of the Daily Mirror.

Pic: Historic Newspapers

Teddy Kennedy's battered Oldsmobile Delta 88
is dragged out of the water at Chappaquiddick.
Pic: Historic Newspapers

The girl who died

Mary Jo Kopechne (above), the girl who died in the car driven by Teddy Kennedy after a party. Next Saturday, she was due to attend another party — to celebrate her 29th birthday.

Car that killed her

Kennedy's battered car (left) after being dragged up from the island saltwater pond into which it plunged.

CHAPPAQUIDDICK:
The car crash that haunted a Kennedy

The location – Chappaquiddick – stays in the mind even if you forget the name of the woman in the car. Between 11.30pm and 1am on the humid moonlit night of Friday July 18, 1969, a black Oldsmobile Delta 88 careered off a bridge on an obscure New England island and plunged into a tidal pond. The driver was Edward Moore Kennedy, 37, and a United States Senator – the sole surviving heir to the Kennedy political dynasty. Kennedy escaped from the Oldsmobile but his only passenger, Mary Jo Kopechne, 28, drowned. Kennedy fled the scene, leaving Mary Jo to suffocate, and didn't report the accident to the police until 10am the next day. His actions have haunted him ever since, thwarting his presidential ambitions despite the immense influence of the Kennedy clan.

"He fled the scene leaving Mary Jo to suffocate and didn't report the accident to the police until 10am the next day – it has haunted him ever since, thwarting his presidential ambitions despite the immense influence of the Kennedy clan."

ALBERT CAMUS:
Absurd death for a French philosopher

If, as Albert Camus said, death is the only certainty, there were worse places to confront it than the opulent interior of a Facel Vega. More than 40 years on, it is still best remembered as the car that killed Camus, existentialist novelist, philosopher and Nobel Prize winner, aged 47, on a foggy afternoon in France in January 1960.

The driver was Michel Gallimard, the car's owner and Camus' publisher. He was famous for driving fast and the Facel Vega was the most powerful car made in France, where its price as a luxury item was loaded hugely with tax. Gallimard was one of the few Frenchmen who could afford one.

> "Camus was thrown back through the rear window where he broke his neck and fractured his skull. He died instantly but it took the police two hours to free his body from the wreck of the Facel."

Camus, a white French Algerian, was hitching a lift with Gallimard, his wife, daughter and their dog from his home in Lourmarin to Paris around 450 miles away. In Camus' leather briefcase was the uncompleted *Premier Homme*, published more than 30 years later.

Death came on a flat and straight stratch when the car swerved, skidded and hit a tree.

'There can be nothing more scandalous than the death of a child, nothing more absurd than to die in a car accident' Albert Camus.
Pic: Historic Newspapers

Movie idol James Dean with his Little Bastard.

Pic: Pictorial Press

JAMES DEAN:
Giant star lived fast, died young

The James Dean crash led to a mass of conspiracy theories. Some said Dean's Porsche 550 Spyder was evil; that it was haunted; that it would curse all who came near it. A premonition of Dean's demise had come from Sir Alec Guinness, who when dining with his fellow actor on a visit to Hollywood, warned he would be dead if he drove his new car. One theory is that Dean was not wearing his spectacles when, on the evening of September 30, 1955, at Cholame, California, his Porsche crashed headlong into a white Ford Tudor making a left turn across his path from Route 41 onto Route 466. The Ford's driver, a student, was slightly injured and later cleared by a court; the neck of James Byron Dean was broken and he died almost instantly, aged 24. The 550 Spyder had been the latest in a succession of cars, starting with a '39 Chevrolet when he was 18 and progressing to a '54 MG and his first Porsche, a 1955 356 Super Speedster convertible. Dean, an avid motorcyclist and car lover, could afford to buy what he wanted as *Giant* and his other films had established him as a superstar. His Porsche – nicknamed "Little Bastard" by Dean – seems to have vanished circa 1960.

"In fact one of the premonitions of Dean's demise came from Sir Alec Guinness, who when dining with the young actor on a visit to Hollywood, warned Dean that he would be dead if he drove his new car."

ERNIE KOVACS:
He died in a fun lovin' family wagon

At around 1.30am on January 13, 1962, a brand-new Chevrolet Corvair 700 Lakewood skidded as it made the turn from Beverly Glen to Santa Monica Boulevard in Los Angeles, crashing head first into a telegraph pole. The driver, 42-year-old comedian Ernie Kovacs, was killed instantly. If Kovacs is remembered at all by the average Briton, it is usually a recollection of a big American character actor with a moustache who gave excellent performances in *Our Man in Havana* and *Operation Mad Ball*. By contrast, American entertainers such as Steve Martin have cited the TV work of the actor/writer/comedian as a major influence, and he has been the subject of at least one TV biopic. One oft-quoted theory to the cause of Kovac's crash is that he lost control of the Corvair while lighting one of his trademark cigars. The Lakewood is the now rare station wagon version of the Series I Corvair. Chevrolet claimed that its undeniably stylish estate car was a 'fun lovin' family wagon' and that it 'handled like a dream'. As early as 1959, magazines such as *Car & Driver* were using other terms to describe the Corvair's roadholding.

> "One oft-quoted theory to the cause of Kovac's crash is that he lost control of the Corvair while lighting one of his trademark cigars."

Smoking kills: the fatal result of trying
to light a cigar while driving a Corvair.
Pic: Historic Newspapers

How Mike Hawthorn's car came to
end up like this remains a mystery.
Pic: Historic Newspapers

MIKE HAWTHORN:
Mystery race crash on the Hogs Back

On a wet and windy day in January 1959, world champion racing driver Mike Hawthorn crashed his Jaguar and died in an accident that has never been fully explained. Driving his modified 3.4 litre saloon along the Hogs Back (part of the A3 in southern England), Hawthorn encountered his friend Rob Walker driving a Mercedes-Benz 300SL, registered ROB 2. An impromptu race ensued as the cars accelerated together to 100mph down the rain-soaked hill. Hawthorn overtook the Mercedes on a left-hand curve and then, going into the right-hander that followed, the Jaguar started to slide, spun, then careered backwards across the carriageway, disappearing from Walker's view. It clipped a traffic island and a truck before coming to rest wrapped around a tree as it disappeared in a cloud of mud and water. The car was almost split in two and Hawthorn died after a couple of minutes as a result of a fractured skull. There has been much speculation about the cause of the crash. Some said Hawthorn, who had kidney problems, suffered a blackout. Others that the car's differential had locked up; that a brake had seized, locked on; or that some part of an alleged non-standard hand throttle failed and allowed the engine to overspeed.

"It then clipped a traffic island and a truck before coming to rest wrapped around a tree as it disappeared in a cloud of mud and water."

PARRY THOMAS:
Grim end to an adventure on Pendine Sands

Welshman Parry Thomas, former chief engineer at Leyland Motors, was an underdog land speed record challenger to Malcolm Campbell and Henry Seagrave in the mid-1920s. With limited funds, he entered the arena with the Higham Special bought from the estate of Count Louis Zborowsky, killed during an Italian Grand Prix. Powered by a 27-litre American Liberty V12 aero engine, it had reached 116mph in Zborowsky's hands but Thomas fitted a more streamlined body, four Zenith carbs, special pistons and a Leyland front axle. He mounted his assault on Pendine Sands in South Wales on April 27, 1926, becoming the first to set two world records on two consecutive days, raising the speed to 171.02mph. By February the following year, Campbell had upped the stakes to 174.88mph, so Thomas returned to Pendine seeking the magic 180. March 3, 1927, was wet and miserable and Babs, as he called the car, crashed. Thomas was killed instantly when the drive chain snapped and Babs was buried in the sand, but disinterred by an enthusiast in 1960.

> "The drive chain had snapped, slashed through its safety guard and killed Thomas instantly."

The mangled remains of Babs lie on a beach
where it was buried but later disinterred.
Pic: Classic Cars

Light front-end panel damage on the
comrade's Silver Shadow after a slight
disagreement with a truck.
Pic: Tim Slade

LEONID BREZHNEV:
Wrote off his armoured Silver Shadow

Leonid Brezhnev, the former USSR president, enjoyed three hobbies: pigeons, hunting and cars. Numerous presidents, prime ministers and kings gave him cars as gifts and he probably had a collection of 15, although some sources say 50. He had access to the latest and biggest Zil but often preferred to drive a blue Lincoln or a black Mercedes to his office in the Kremlin, where he arrived at exactly 9 o'clock every morning. One of his favourites was an armoured Rolls-Royce Silver Shadow given to him by American President Richard Nixon. His driving career came to an end in 1980 when he steered out of an official parade in Moscow and into an oncoming truck. The Rolls-Royce now lives in an automobile museum in Riga, capital of the former soviet state Latvia (now an independent democracy). Behind the wheel of the mangled Roller is a wax model of the startled First secretary, which looks more like former British foreign secretary Dennis Healey.

"His driving career came to an end in 1980 when he steered out of an official parade and into an oncoming truck in Moscow."

SAMMY DAVIS JUNIOR:
Lost an eye in a Cadillac crash

Driving to Los Angeles in November 1954, the diminutive but dynamic song-and-dance entertainer Sammy Davis Junior crashed his huge convertible Cadillac into on coming traffic in an attempt to avoid a car that was making a U-turn directly in front of him. This was long before the days of airbags and, in the collision, his head hit the steering wheel. Sticking out of the centre of the wheel was a piece of ornamental chrome and Davis lost his left eye. Davis was, with Frank Sinatra and Dean Martin, one of the Rat Pack and once said: 'I haven't done badly for a one-eyed, black Jewish dwarf.'

"He crashed attempting to avoid a car that was making a u-turn."

A *Stutz* was the luxobarge of choice for porn film producers and
any slightly dated all-rounders; Sammy had to have one.
Pic: Martin Buckley Archive

McCartney in that staple choice for the '60s
man-about-town – a Radford Mini Cooper.
Pic: Pictorial Press

PAUL MCCARTNEY:
Spent £70,000 on Lambo in the pond

Sir Paul had a bit of a thing about Lamborghinis for a while and his first was a 400GT in 1967. He also owned an Espada and, the story goes, someone phoned about an ad for the car. The owner's secretary picked the phone up and said: 'Come and have a look,' giving him directions to an address. When he got there, it was McCartney selling the car. He showed him around the car – red, with a fairly hideous matching red interior. He was quite taken with it, was getting on well with the ex-Beatle, and about to make an offer when McCartney said: 'Look, I don't want to sell it to you. I like you and, to be honest, it's not a good car.' It turned out that Linda McCartney had left it parked one night with the handbrake off and it had rolled into a pond. After three days, Sir Paul pulled it out because a Lambo in the lake isn't very ecological. Because of some kind of emotional attachment to it, he had the Lambo rebuilt for around £70,000. 'But, if you want a Lamborghini that's mint, and has never been in a pond,' he said, 'this isn't the one.'

"After three days, Sir Paul pulled it out because a Lambo in the lake isn't very ecological."

OJ SIMPSON:
Gave Ford and its Bronco unwanted publicity

OJ Simpson will forever be associated with the Ford Bronco, giving the car maker its most unwanted degree of publicity since the heyday of the Pinto. Before June 1994, those aware of OJ were mainly fans of *The Naked Gun* and various 1970s epics of the Klansman, *The Towering Inferno* and *The Cassandra Crossing* school of cinema. Then the bodies of Nicole Simpson – OJ's ex-wife – and her friend Ronald Goodman were found outside the Simpson condominium in Los Angeles. Four days later, the LAPD issued an arrest warrant for OJ on the two counts of murder with special circumstances and, as OJ did not surrender, he was declared a fugitive at large. That evening, the crew of a patrol car noticed a white 1994-model Ford Bronco owned by Simpson's friend Al Cowlings, with a familiar figure in the passenger seat. The Bronco was driven slowly for 60 miles to OJ's house with the suspect holding a gun to his own head. Simpson was arrested and his trial attracted worldwide attention until he was cleared of murder.

> "The Bronco was driven slowly for 60 miles to OJ's house with the suspect holding a gun to his own head."

Maybe if OJ had used Bill Harrah's Jerrari – a
Jeep Wagoneer crossed with a Ferrari 365 –
the police would never have caught him.
Pic: Road & Track magazine

The **Rover P6** is one of the world's safest cars – unless you forget
to turn the steering wheel on a dangerous mountain bend.

Pic: Pictorial Press

GRACE KELLY:
Final cliffhanger for the icy blonde

Driving a Sunbeam Alpine, Grace Kelly shot some of her most famous scenes in the Hitchcock thriller *To Catch a Thief* on the winding mountain roads above the principality of Monaco she would later rule. Tragically she died on the same road; on September 13, 1982, Princess Grace and her daughter Princess Stephanie were travelling in their Rover 3500S which careered off one of the winding roads leading to Monaco. At the time, the Rover was one of the world's most robust cars but its crumple zones were of little use when tumbling down a cliffside. Princess Stephanie was able to get out of the car when it finally stopped rolling, and suffered only a few injuries. Princess Grace wasn't so lucky: the 52-year-old former Hollywood film star had suffered a mild stroke that caused her to lose control of the car. She was found unconscious at the foot of the cliff and died in hospital the next day.

"The 3500S Rover was one of the world's most robust cars in an accident but its crumple zones weren't much use when it was tumbling down the side of a cliffside."

Daily Mirror

4d. Monday, December 19, 1966 ◆ ◆ ◆ No. 19,592

Guinness heir's Lotus 'disintegrated' in cras[h]

DEATH CAR

Dartmoor warders in plea to Mitchell

By DOUGLAS SLIGHT

AN appeal to runaway prisoner Frank Mitchell goes out today—from a group of warders at Dartmoor jail.

The warders think that 37-year-old Mitchell, who escaped from a Dartmoor outside working party last Monday, might want to give himself up by now. Yesterday, they asked the Daily Mirror to publish this plea to Mitchell:

If you let us know where to meet you, we will be quite willing to pick you up.

One prison officer told me: "It is quite on the cards that Mitchell is keen to get back, but frightened to give himself up to the police.

"We think he would be far more inclined to give himself up to people who know him and he knows he can trust."

Meeting

"We appeal to him to get in touch with your paper, so that we can bring the matter to a close without anyone getting hurt."

This unofficial offer is likely to be supported by the local Prison Officers' Association branch at a meeting tonight.

A statement which the group of warders issued last night said:

"Despite contrary statements made by people outside the prison, there is a feeling among prison officers that Mitchell will not be offering any violence.

"During his absence there has been no report of any crime, nor indeed any sighting of him since he was reported missing.

"Prison officers believe he might easily surrender to someone he trusts. There is a growing feeling among the prison staff that Mitchell, wrongly, of course, may be trying to prove something.

Trusted

"He may surrender to a member of the prison service, and thus prove himself to be the person those in charge of Dartmoor believe he had grown to be."

The statement added: "If he does this, he will not only gain reasonable consideration for himself, but will also vindicate those who trusted him and were proved wrong—and prove wrong, indeed, those who have condemned him."

GORDON GREGOR reports:

Detectives seeking Mitchell in the East End of London believe that he is being helped by gangsters who value a man of his size, strength and violent past—as a "frightener."

Mitchell—he is 6ft. 1in. tall and weighs 16st.—was serving a life sentence in Dartmoor for an axe attack on an elderly couple while he was on the run in 1958 from Broadmoor mental institution. He had also escaped from Rampton institution.

Big jail shake-up.—See Page 4.

Torn and twisted. The crashed Lotus Elan ... testimony to the horror in which Tara Browne died.

Was Tara killed in bi[d] to save his girl

By PAUL HUGHES and BRIAN McCONNELL

TARA Browne, 21 - year - old heir to a Guinness fortune, is dead.

He was killed, probably, because of his gallantry.

His 110 - mile - an - hour Lotus Elan sports car crashed into the back of a parked van early yesterday.

Tara is believed to have swung the car in the last seconds before the impact to protect his passenger, pretty 19-year-old model Suki Potier.

She was shocked but uninjured.

Two hours later, in St. Stephen's Hospital Fulham, the battle to save Tara was finally lost.

He died with everything to live for ... days after talking of his hopes of a reconciliation with his wife, 24-year-old Nicky Macsberry.

Shocked

Suki, too shocked to talk of the crash, was given drugs yesterday at her home in Knightsbridge.

Her father, Mr. Gilbert Potier, said: "He saved my daughter's life, I am convinced of that.

"It appears that he swung the car in an attempt to save Suki from the full force of the crash.

"It was a very gallant act. It's tragic it should have cost him his life."

Tara, mop-haired, controversial, a friend of top pop singers, was due to inherit £1,000,000 when he was twenty-five.

He crashed in South Kensington while driving Suki home.

Mr. Charles Corneille, manager of the Phoenix Theatre, heard the crash as he lay reading in bed in his flat.

"I saw the driver pinned like a doll in the wrecked car," he said. "There was not much we could do for him."

A neighbour, Mr. Frederick Moysey, said: "I saw the girl passenger running about in the road, waving her arms.

"The car virtually disintegrated. The steering

Continued on Back Page

Suki Potier . . . She escaped from the crash with shock.

Tara . . . heir to [the] Guinness fortune

TARA BROWNE:
Last day in the life of an heir

Few people are afforded the honour of having their accidents immortalised in song lyrics, especially those written by Beatles John Lennon and Paul McCartney. Then again, Tara Browne was no ordinary young man. An aristocrat (his father was Lord Aranmore-and-Browne, his mother Oonagh Guinness, heir to the brewery fortune) he was a London 'face' in the Swinging Sixties who partied hard, counting McCartney among his close friends. At the time of his accident 21-year-old Browne was living with model Suki Potier at London's posh Ritz Hotel and was four years away from inheriting a fortune. On December 18, 1966, Browne was driving down Redcliffe Gardens in Earls Court, London, during the early hours, when a Volkswagen pulled out of a side street into his path. In swerving to avoid it, his Lotus Elan ploughed into a stationary van. He was pronounced dead from head injuries on arrival at hospital. Suki Potier escaped with bruises and shock and that Lennon/McCartney song lives on 'A day in the life', on the Beatles' *Sgt. Peppers Lonely Hearts Club Band* album.

> "In swerving to avoid a VW, his Lotus Elan ploughed into a stationary van."

Lotus crash headlines that inspired part of the lyrics to 'A day in the life'.
Pic: Historic Newspapers

SIR STIRLING MOSS:
Ogle designed his 'wet dream car'

The off-track motoring adventures of Stirling Moss involved being banned for speeding in 1960, providing certain traffic police officers with a deeply annoying catchphrase (remember the TV ad for the Renault 20TS?) and having Ogle design his own 'dream car' – a custom-designed Ford Cortina Mk I coupé. He later referred to it as his 'wet dream car' which is pretty harsh, although some would say its looks were far inferior to Ford's own 'Saxon' project for a Mk.1 Cortina Coupe. He also rolled a BMW Isetta bubble car on its launch (probably not difficult as the car was not known for its stability).

"He also rolled a BMW Isetta bubble car on its launch (probably not difficult as the car was't known for its stability)."

**Facel Vega boss George Abecasis (left) hands Stirling Moss
the keys to his new HK500, still his favourite road car.**

Pic: Martin Buckley Archive

Ghosted picture showing the two A-Series engines of John Cooper's twin-engined Mini Cooper, the car that almost killed him. Pic: Classic Cars

JOHN COOPER:
Two engines were more than enough

Twin-engined vehicles always sound like a good way of getting more power onto the road but have been fraught with problems. John Cooper was badly injured on the A3 Kingston bypass in the south of England in 1962 when driving his twin-engined Mini Cooper. Cooper and his team had made their mark in Formula 1, 2 and 3 and in 1961 took the cars to America to race at Indianapolis. Cooper's BMC Formula 3 car shared the same A-series engine that was later used in the Mini. In the 1960s, Mini Coopers won the Monte Carlo and other international rallies. The car in the 1962 crash had been raced in Sicily's Targa Florio round a daunting 92-mile circuit not designed for autos, with hairpin bends that had sheer drops on one side. The twin-engined car was a typical Cooper lash-up, with the same front sub-frames fitted at both ends. According to his ghosted autobiography Grand Prix Carpet Bagger: '[At the rear...] we had removed the rack and used the steering links as another suspension arm which pivoted on the sub-frame. Unfortunately it was one of those steering links that let go.' The ball joint on the end of the link had been secured to the sub-frame instead of the rack itself. As a result, a rear wheel 'suddenly made a sharp right turn', said Cooper later. The car was a write-off, and Cooper badly injured, but he eventually made a full recovery.

> "The car, which had been raced in the Targa Florio, was a typical Cooper lash-up, with the same front sub-frames fitted at both ends."

Mr Demetriou trying hard not to look like a gangster. Which he wasn't.
Pic: *Car* magazine

FRIXOS DEMETRIOU:
Stored imported cars behind casino kitchen

Frixos Demetriou, the Cypriot casino owner, wasn't a guy who hung around when he'd had a good idea. While awaiting a flight connection he spotted a Fiat Gamine roadster that looked like Noddy's car based on the Fiat 500. Frixos reckoned he could sell a few in the UK.

In Turin he met Alfredo Vignale, designer of the Gamine and bought 200 cars in cash – and then did a similar deal with Francis Lombardi for his 850 coupe-based Grand Prix. He booked a stand at the 1968 Earls Court London motor show and was soon importing 100 cars a month, storing them in a shed behind the kitchens of his casino..

By 1970 Frixos wasn't that fussed about selling cars. To shift some stock he sent a shipment of 100 cars to Cyprus. Many of them still survive – apart from his own car, that is. It was there, in 1970, sitting in the back of a Samantha, that Frixos Demetriou met his end: a runaway British army tank flattened his car – and him.

> "He booked a stand at the 1968 Earls Court London motor show and was soon importing 100 cars a month"

car

JANUARY 1969 3 shillings

meet the
Racing Car Show's
least enthusiastic

A cad and a Jag are never far apart.
Alan Clark surveys XJ40s ready for export.
Pic: Martin Buckley archive

ALAN CLARK:
Alpine rallyist who appreciated the Velox

Barrister, historian, diarist, possible Nazi-sympathiser and avid *Viz* reader... Alan Clark's favourite roles appear to have been those of 'cad, bounder and rotter'. He was one of the more intriguing advertisements for the benefits of the public school system but Clark had other pastimes – such as motoring. Readers of his infamous diaries will already have learned Alan's opinions on Carabineri drivers ('spastic bum-boys') and discovered that a stricken Aston Martin V8 Vantage 'is always good for a laugh'. However, the Clark motoring career encompassed racing Nulbar Gulbenkian in an SS100, owning vehicles as varied as a DS Decapotable; Austins Seven, Sheerline and Atlantic; a D-Type, an E-Type, and a Continental S. He took part in the Alpine Rallies of 1973 and 1993 and Clark's columns for *Classic Car* were some of the best written of the entire genre. They revealed why Italian cars were his particular bête noire, which might well explain the diary entry above, and a genuine appreciation of cars as varied as the XK-Series Jaguars (appropriately enough, a model forever associated with Terry-Thomas in 1950s films) and the E-Series Vauxhall Velox.

> **"Readers of his infamous diaries will already have learned Alan's opinion's on Carabineri drivers ('spastic bum-boys') and discovered that a stricken Aston Martin DBS Vantage 'is always good for a laugh."**

The stunt driver scrubbed-up quite well for this shot.

Pic: Martin Buckley Archive

CITROEN SM:
Cool supercar too sharp for Contessa

Despite its trendy image, Citroen's SM supercar appeared in few films or TV series but perhaps the most memorable was *The Protectors*, one of the last in a long tradition of action series from Lew Grade's British TV stable. It starred Robert Vaughn, while Nyree Dawn Porter provided female glamour as the Contessa Di Contini, a wealthy aristocrat with a taste for fast cars. Citroen's publicity department provided the SM but Porter refused to drive it because she found the steering and brakes too sharp. All the shots in the series are of a Citroen driver in a wig.

The great, the good and sometimes the not-so-good lined up to buy the super-cool SM in the pre-fuel crisis years – personalities as diverse as Graham Greene, Johan Cruyff, Mike Hailwood, Lee J Cobb (the teamster boss from *On the Waterfront*), Lee Majors (*The Six Million Dollar Man*) and even Leonid Brezhnev and Idi Amin.

Magician/comedian Paul Daniels was pulled up by the police when speeding in his SM. As the officer approached the car, Daniels made his Citroen Maserati rise and fall on its suspension repeatedly by manipulating the height control lever next to the seat. When the policeman asked him what was wrong with car he said 'It's out of breath, it's panting...'

"Citroen's publicity department provided the SM for Nyree Dawn Porter – which was great except she refused to drive it"

DICTATORS' CARS AND REGAL CHOICES

For royal personages and heads of state only

There are certain protocols to be observed if the world is to regard you as a deranged dictator of quality; awarding yourself the Victoria Cross, custom-designing your very own Air Field Marshall of the Fleet uniform and shooting members of the opposition is a pretty good start. But that cheque from your American/Russian/Chinese/British/French paymasters is burning a hole in your pocket. You need a car that inspires awe and/or naked fear in your loyal countrymen and furthermore, one that will hide the fact that you stand 5ft 3ins in your stilted feet. There can be only one choice – the Mercedes-Benz 600 Laundette.

The 600, although also used by the Pope and other eminent personages, is the Mercedes-Benz that will be forever associated with Idi Amin, Papa Doc Duvalier, Nicolai Ceausescu and any other world leader who appears to have strayed from the pages of Greene or Le Carré. Other models have become equally associated with world leaders, from the Humber Super Snipes of Harold Macmillan's British Conservative government to De Gaulle's beloved Citroen DS, and West German leader Konrad Adenauer's 300d four-door cabriolet.

ARGENTINIAN FORD FALCON:
Transport for the midnight death squads

A minor pleasure for western motor enthusiasts is consulting the *World Car Year Book* and sniggering in post-modern ironic fashion at the products of the Developing World. There are the usual suspects – the Hindustan Ambassador and the Peykan Hi-Line; then there was the 1960s Ford Falcon. Argentina built them from 1963 to 1991. Of course there were cosmetic updates – later models could be had with Granada Ghia-type alloy wheels – but the net effect was the same as GAZ's attempts to ring the changes on the Volga M22. Still, a total of nearly 500,000 Falcons were built in Argentina and there was even a Borgward-diesel engineered version for masochists. The Falcon was Argentina's car for the farmers, businessmen and military. Especially the military.

Following the coup d'état of 1976, *grupos del terror* (police and military death squads) operated from a network of 360 secret detention centres. Having a similar name to a suspected liberal could be enough to warrant a midnight visit in black Ford Falcons devoid of livery or even licence number.

Not a car you want to see pulling up outside your house late at night.
Pic: Martin Buckley Archive

"The Falcon was Argentina's car for the farmers, businessmen and military. Especially the military."

ADOLF HITLER:
Mercedes played part in his rise to power

"Mercedes-Benz automobiles were seen as symbols of the prosperous Germany promised by the Nazis, and were often displayed by party leaders."

It is an aspect of its history Mercedes would not like us to dwell on but Daimler Benz cars were a favourite of Adolf Hitler and played their part in his rise to power. Mercedes were symbols of the prosperous Germany promised by the Nazis, and often displayed by party leaders. The vast eight-cylinder limousines, with both open and closed bodywork, were fast and strong, allowing Hitler and top associates to campaign throughout Germany at a speed that caught his political opponents napping. State power brought almost infinite resources to the Nazi Party and liberal use of luxury Mercedes limousines was a perk of the job. Hitler, who never learned to drive, purchased a 16-horsepower Mercedes in December 1924 after serving nine months of a five-year sentence for treason. The leader of the temporarily banned Nazi Party hoped his chauffeur-driven car would impress his previous followers and persuade doubters of his political importance.

They say little men like big cars: Adolf with the mother and fatherland of all Mercedes limousines.
Pic: Pictorial Press

Exotica jostles for position in
Perón's underground parking facility
Pic: Pictorial Press

JUAN PERÓN:
Fangio was in his racing team

The picture shows the type of vehicles that any self-respecting exiled South American president would be proud to have in his fleet but they represent only a part of Juan Perón's collection. The motorsport enthusiast who was twice president of Argentina (1946-55 and 1973-74) favoured a cream 1939 Packard Straight 8 convertible in the 1940s. In 1952, he took delivery of the last Ferrari built with coachwork by Ghia of Turin – a black and yellow coupé-bodied 212 Inter. In 1949, Peron funded the establishment of the Equipe Argentina motor racing team: he loved sport and had a particular fondness for motor racing. The driver of the Maserati 4CLT, in its national colours of blue and yellow, was the legendary Juan-Manuel Fangio. Another post-war Maserati racer from Argentina, Alejandro de Tomaso, had to leave the country in 1955 following his part in an attempted anti-Perón coup. Perón died in 1974.

"The motorsport enthusiast who was twice president of Argentina favoured a cream 1939 Packard Straight 8 convertible."

SHAH OF IRAN:
Rolls-Royce collector built the Peykan

Throughout his 38-year reign, the last Shah of Iran was an avid collector of Rolls-Royces, owning a Silver Ghost, a Twenty, a 20/25, a 25/30, Phantoms I – III, a brace of Phantom IVs and a blue Corniche. He also bought the first left-hand drive Camargue, demonstrating there is no accounting for taste. Rumours that his late Imperial Majesty owned a fleet of some 3,000 cars were vehemently denied by his secretary but the royal garages did include a Ferrari 500 Superfast, a 1971 Lamborghini Miura SVJ (subsequently acquired by actor Nicolas Cage) and a Tipo 103 Maserati 5000GT. The French government gave him a 1939 Bugatti 57C as a wedding present. In 1967, the Shah officially opened the assembly lines of the 'Peykan' ('medium-sized car') at the Iranian National Auto plant. The Peykan, better known in the UK as the Hillman Hunter, was exported in kit-form from the Rootes Group plant in the UK. In the 1970s, the Peykan survived both Chrysler's control of the Rootes Group and the fall of the Shah's regime in 1979. *Car* magazine referred to 'the mad mullahs of Iran' but the Peykan was at one time Britain's number one exported car.

"Rumours that his late Imperial Majesty owned a fleet of some 3,000 cars were vehemently denied by his secretary."

The last Shah of Iran, in shades, test drives a Jaguar E-Type.
Pic: Martin Buckley Archive

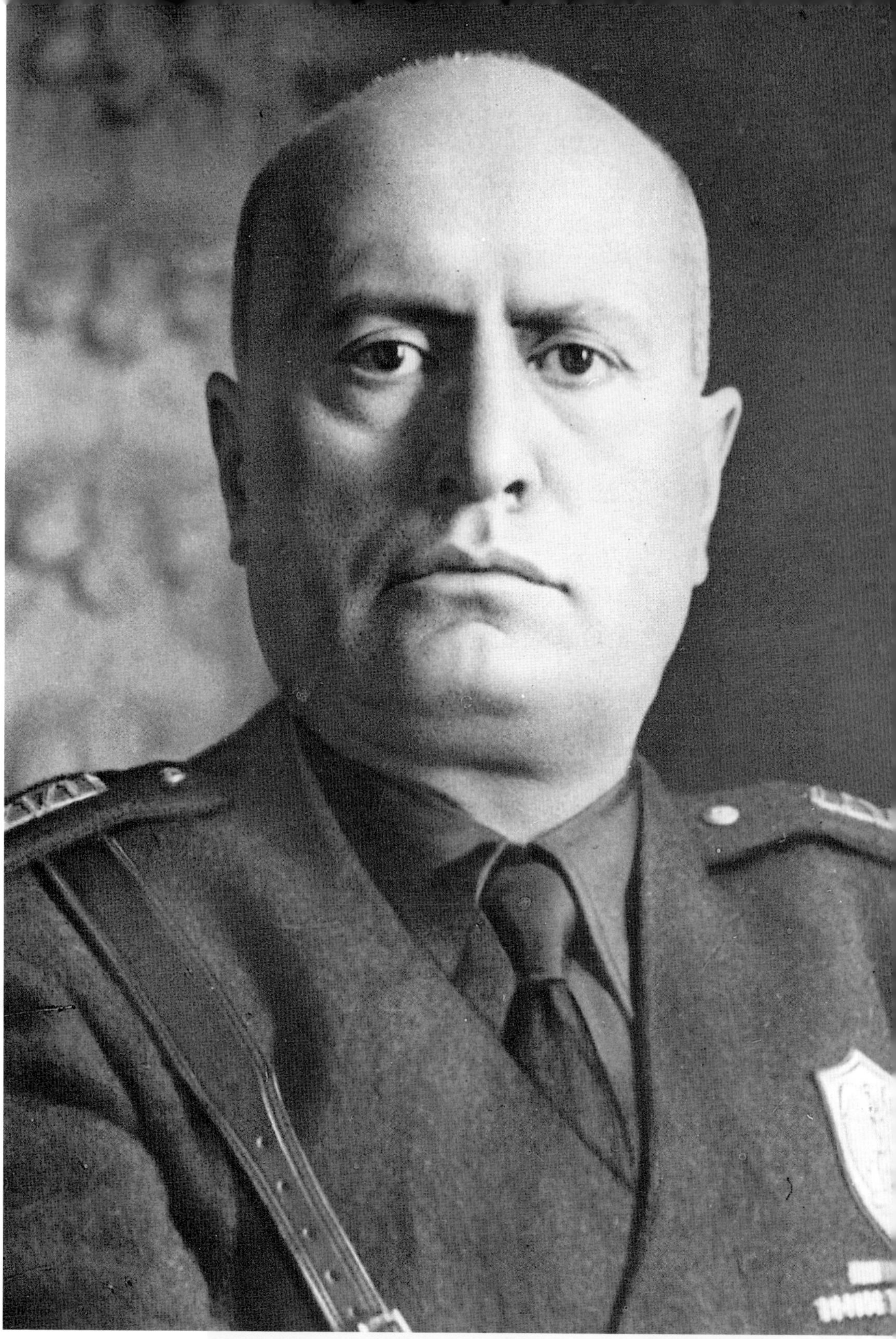

BENITO MUSSOLINI:
Ordered red leather trim for his mistress

In 1940 Benito Mussolini, the Italian Fascist dictator, wanted to buy a car for his mistress Claretta. He walked into his local Fiat dealer and ordered a Fiat 2800 with beautiful Touring bodywork – black with red leather: Il Duce was an Alfa man and a keen motorist. Claretta couldn't drive but the official mistress to Italy's leading Fascist was given her own government chauffeur. But Mussolini was doing the driving in April 1945 when, in a bid to escape the Allies, he drove the Fiat towards Chiavenna where a plane was waiting to take the pair to Switzerland. They never made it: partisans shot dead their 16-strong escort and Mussolini and Claretta were executed. Their bodies were displayed in Milan but the car had much better luck. The partisans pushed it into Lake Garda but it was retrieved and smuggled into Switzerland under bales of hay in a railway car. It lived a quiet life until 1980 when, restored to immaculate condition, it was sold at an auction in Geneva.

"The partisans pushed the Fiat 2800 into Lake Garda but it was retrieved and smuggled into Switzerland in a railway car."

Benito Mussolini: a look to put pushy
car salesmen in their place.
Pic: Pictorial Press

CHARLES DE GAULLE:
Assassins foiled by lucky black DS

"As dusk fell over Paris, de Gaulle's black Citroen DS was speeding down the Avenue de la Liberation at 70mph when 12 OAS men opened fire on the car."

Terrorists of the OAS – the Secret Army Organisation – made their second attempt on the life of President Charles de Gaulle on August 22, 1962. The leader of France was being chauffeured in a black Citroen DS.

The OAS believed de Gaulle had betrayed France by yielding Algeria to nationalists earlier that year. As dusk fell over Paris, de Gaulle's DS was speeding down the Avenue de la Libération at 70mph when 12 OAS men opened fire. They saw the open-fire signal too late and most of their bullets hit the Citroen from behind, bursting its tyres and causing it to go into a front-wheel skid. Some bullets shattered the rear window as the chauffeur wrestled with the wheel and accelerated out of the skid. De Gaulle and his wife emerged unscathed by keeping their heads down, and thanks to its hydropneumatic suspension, the DS was able to limp safely to Villacoublay where a helicopter was waiting to take the de Gaulles to their country retreat. These events were the basis for Frederick Forsyth's book *The Day of the Jackal* which was made into a film.

When this picture was taken, de Gaulle (right)
would have been an easy target for an assassin.
Pic: Pictorial Press

Dacia's UK image makers brought new meaning to the
phrase 'damning with faint praise' when they tagged the new
Renault 12-based saloon 'very acceptable'. But to whom?
Pic: Martin Buckley Archive

NICHOLAI CEAUSESCU:
Suit and trilby in a beautiful Laundette

There are certain conventions surrounding any dictator worth his salt: kitsch art images of yourself at every street corner, one or more mistresses as members of the cabinet and a psychotic playboy as no.1 son. If you've appointed yourself president of an eastern European state, wearing suit and trilby combinations specially designed to make you resemble a B-movie mobster is another.

Nicholai Ceausescu, the Romanian dictator (1918-89), fulfilled most of these criteria with the bonus of being rather short and having a Mercedes-Benz 600 Laundette as his state car. An open car is far superior to a limousine if you wish to wave at your adoring public and Nicholai employed several gentlemen with dark glasses to ensure such universal adoration.

Lesser citizens of Romania had to make do with the cast-off Renault Dacia Denim which was marketed under the catchy tag line 'very acceptable.'

"Naturally a 600 Laundette is far superior to a limousine if you wish to wave at your adoring public and Nicholai employed several gentlemen with dark glasses to ensure such universal adoration."

IDI AMIN:
And other charming Mercedes 600 owners

The list of Mercedes-Benz 600 enthusiasts is truly impressive: they include Queen Elizabeth II, Mao Tse Tung and Idi Amin.

After seizing power from the Ugandan president Milton Obote in 1971, Idi Amin, one of the few politicians to have both advised the Queen on etiquette and to tell Israeli premier Golda Meir to 'pack her knickers', embarked on a political career that would see the death of more than 300,000 Ugandans. Awarding himself various medals and university degrees was not enough for Idi – an international statesman deserved only the best vehicles and like all world's most successful despots, the car of choice was the indomitable Mercedes 600. One of the last Pullman limousines was supplied to the government of Iraq in 1981 and Mao Tse Tung is alleged to have owned 25 of them.

Naturally Leonid Brezhnev was an enthusiast and, opposite, we see the Queen out for a spin with Romanian dictator Nicholai Ceausescu. The German government still uses a five-ton armoured Pullman for particularly honoured heads of state. Idi ordered two 600s in 1976 and 182 of the cars are attributed to the continent of Africa.

Idi owned two Citroen SMs and rallied one of them which must have been one of the more awesome spectacles in motor racing history.

"Idi even rallied one of the SMs, which must have been one of the more awesome spectacles in motor racing history."

The Queen in a Mercedes 600 Laundette.

Pic: Pictorial Press

The vast Daimler Straight Eight limousine used by
King George VI on the 1947 tour of South Africa.
Pic: Classic Cars

DAIMLER'S ROYAL DEMISE:
Visual motoring trademark until the 1960s

By the time of King Edward VIII's abdication in 1936, the large, sombre and silent Daimler limousines with their massive bonnets – housing appropriately huge straight-eight engines – had become one of the best known visual trademarks of British royalty and colonial power. Daimler kept a reserve fleet of 'royal stock' cars for use on tours. Typically the royals would be in an open Daimler with the entourage of 'ladies in waiting' and the like following behind in closed limousines. Daimler was a British company, of course, and using a car from a foreign manufacturer would have been unthinkable.

Interestingly though, Edward was using a Canadian-built Buick for private business at the time of the abdication scandal. The Queen was brought up on Daimlers and the Queen Mother remained faithful to the marque to the end. But the royal household's loyalty to Daimler as

> "Daimler kept a reserve fleet of 'royal stock' cars for use on tours."

a principal state vehicle was becoming strained by the time Queen Elizabeth II was crowned due to the exploits of Lady Docker, the flamboyant wife of Daimler boss Sir Bernard Docker. Daimler was to remain the official royal car until well into 1950s, but by the early '60s the marque had been ousted from the Royal Mews.

ROYAL ROLLERS:
Highroof line for Royal hierarchy

In 1961 two new Rolls-Royce Phantom Vs went into service with the British Royal Household for day-to-day state duties, be it driving silently in a procession at 10mph or cruising down a motorway with a brace of Royal Protection Squad outriders to a factory opening. Code-named Canberra, they had a special high roofline and a perspex section in the rear of the roof that could be covered with a separate panel. They remain the quintessential royal limousines that have travelled the world on royal tours in a 41-year career. In 1978, the Queen was presented with another high-roofed Phantom Rolls-Royce in the Canberra style as a belated Silver Jubilee present from the Society of Motor Manufacturers and Traders. Famously , when visiting McDonald's for a photo opportunity, the car wouldn't fit into the drive-through. The nine state limousines in the Royal Mews consist of one Bentley, five Rolls-Royces and three Daimlers. All are painted in royal maroon livery and the Bentley and Rolls-Royces do not have registration number plates. Lesser mortals – butlers and the like – travel in a fleet of Vauxhall Sintra people carriers.

"This the car which famously, when visiting McDonald's for a photo opportunity, wouldn't fit into the drive-through..."

One of the original Phantom V Canberra-
style limousines on tour in Germany.
Pic: Classic Cars.

PRINCE CHARLES:

Scolded Diana for leaning on his Aston Martin

By the late 1960s Prince Charles was old enough to take the wheel. One of his first private cars was an MGC in 1968 and, of course, he was driven around in a variety of Rolls-Royce and Daimler limousines. His first headline-grabbing car was the Aston Martin DB6 Volante he bought in 1971 and still owns and uses. This was the car over which, years later, he famously scolded Princess Diana – in full view of the TV and press – for leaning against its delicate alloy panels as they watched a polo match. Charles bought another Aston Martin convertible in the '80s. In a cringing display of forelock-tugging toadying, Aston produced a 'Prince of Wales' specification replica.

"This was the car over which, years later, he famously scolded Princess Diana – in full view of the TV and press – for leaning against its delicate alloy panels as they watched a polo match."

Charles collects Princess Anne from hospital in **1971** in his **DB6 Volante**.
Pic: Classic Cars

ROYAL ESTATE CARS:
Windsors liked Teddy boy favourite

When you have a big estate (or several, in this case), then it's always a good idea to have an estate, or shooting break as they used to be called. The royals have always liked big station wagons, being adventurous at times. The Queen Mother owned an American-style Ford Pilot shooting break for use in Scotland. George VI was apparently very fond of the Pilot, specifying a non-standard floor gear-change as he was not a great column-shift enthusiast. In the 1950s and '60s, the royal family's practical motoring and leisure time needs were served by a series of large estate cars that the Queen often drove. A 1956 high-roofed Ford Zephyr, with wooden panelling, was a royal one-off reflecting the Windsor's horsy tastes. The

"The Friary Cresta survives in the mews at Sandringham but not all of the Queen's private cars have met such a happy fate."

1962 Vauxhall Cresta Friary, dream car of millions of Teddy boys, was a standard production car that remained in use until the early '70s, mainly at Windsor. It was often photographed emerging from the car park at a polo match. For fishing trips the Queen had a shooting break version of the Vanden Plas 3-litre with carriers on the roof for angling equipment. The Friary Cresta survives in the mews at Sandringham but the Vanden Plas shooting break was allegedly crashed and scrapped.

The Queen's Vauxhall Cresta Friary Estate at
Windsor in the mid-60s. Pic: Classic Cars

DUKE OF EDINBURGH:
Prototype was his personal transport

In 1965 the Duke of Edinburgh replaced his ageing Lagonda 3 litre with a one-off prototype called the Ogle Triplex GTS that he had seen at the British motor show that year. Based on a Reliant Scimitar it had been commissioned by the glass manufacturers Triplex and designed by Ogle. The Queen's husband was much taken with the car and asked if he could have it on loan as his personal transport. Reliant was more than happy as it raised the profile of a company best known for its three-wheelers. But it wasn't such a good arrangement for Triplex which had paid for the car and was now denied the opportunity to display it around more motor shows. Still it was hard to say 'no' to a Duke and he used the car happily for two years, forging a royal link with Reliant of Tamworth in the English Midlands that would continue for many years.

"But it wasn't such a good arrangement for Triplex who, after all, had paid for the car and were now denied the opportunity to display it around the motor shows."

The Duke with the Scimitar he commandeered from Triplex.
Pic: Classic Cars

PRINCESS ANNE:
Followed her father's taste in cars

The Duke of Edinburgh's Triplex Scimitar obviously left an impression on his daughter. When the time came, in 1970, for Princess Anne to buy a car, she ordered a Reliant Scimitar GTE, a production car inspired by a Triplex one-off. She owned several of these Ford-engined, glassfibre-bodied sports estate cars over the next few years and was famously fined for speeding in one of the early examples in the 1970s. She became such a fan of Reliant that she bought a three-wheel Robin for use on her country estate and later bought a Rover SD1. Anne's most dramatic motoring moment was in 1974 when, returning to Buckingham Palace after an evening out with her husband Captain Mark Phillips, a road was blocked by a gunman in a kidnap attempt. The Vanden Plas limousine was damaged, and the chauffeur and bodyguard injured, but the royal couple emerged unscathed.

"She became such a fan of Reliant that she even bought a three-wheel Robin for use on her country estate."

Rover SD1s were trendy for about five minutes in 1976 so
Princess Anne supplemented her Scimitar GTE with one. She
doesn't look that happy about it though.
Pic: Classic Cars

The Queen's new State Bentley looks like an over-
inflated taxi cab. It also makes her look tiny.
Pic: Bentley Motors

NEW STATE BENTLEY:
Grand car that looks like a giant taxi cab

Britain's new State Bentley was presented to the Queen to mark her Golden Jubilee in May 2002 and, unlike the Rolls-Royce Phantoms based on production models, it is a one-off model conceived by a Bentley-led consortium of British motor industry manufacturers and suppliers. It was the first Bentley to be used for state occasions although other royals have run Bentley Turbos for some time (it was driving a Bentley Turbo that led to Princess Anne's speeding fine in 2001). The state car was designed with input from the Queen, Duke of Edinburgh and the Queen's head chauffeur. Unlike the old Phantoms, the new car has a monocoque construction (no chassis), which means better use can be made of the interior space. The transmission tunnel runs under the floor without encroaching on the cabin, so the stylists could work with a lowered roofline while preserving the proper interior height. The rear doors were designed so the Queen can stand up straight before stepping down to the ground. It's all very admirable but its designers seem to have overlooked one thing: it looks like a giant taxi cab.

"It is a one-off model conceived by a Bentley-led consortium of British motor industry manufacturers and suppliers."

ROYAL RUNABOUTS:
A Cadillac Cyclone was the most flamboyant

The Queen drove smaller 3-litre Daimlers off duty in the 1950s while the Duke of Edinburgh used rakish 3-litre Lagonda and Alvis dropheads in that decade and early '60s. There were less exalted limousines for more work a day royal duties, such as the Vanden Plas Princess 4-litre, that favourite of provincial lord mayors. For Commonwealth duties, a wider variety of vehicles included a brace of Humber Super Snipe cabriolets: a 1948 model and the still-surviving 1953 car used on the 1954 Commonwealth tour. A silver Vanden Plas Princess Laundette carried Princess Margaret at the Jamaican Independence ceremony in 1962 and an unstable-looking Jaguar XJ6 cabriolet was used for the Queen Mother's tour of Tonga in 1972. One of the most flamboyant cars used for a Commonwealth tour was the Cadillac Cyclone, presented by GM-Canada for the royal tour of 1959 – a Cadillac '75 limousine with the *de rigueur* tailfins and a perspex dome over the rear compartment. Subtle it was not. By the early '60s the Queen had come to like the solid values of big 3-litre Rovers and used one of the later 3.5 litre V8 version until well into the '80s.

"By the early 60s the Queen had come to like the solid values of big 3 litre Rovers and used one of the later 3.5 litre V8 versions until well into 80s. To this day it is said to be her favourite car."

To this day one of HM's favourite cars is
the Rover P5: here she is driving one.
Pic: Classic Cars

CZECHOSLOVAKIA'S TATRA:
Vicious behaviour on Hitler's roads

During World War II, legend has it that German officers were under orders not to drive rear-engined Tatras in occupied Czechoslovakia, such was their reputation for vicious and irretrievable oversteer.

With its flush headlights and hunched, slatted rear quarters, this fast and beautifully engineered machine was a vision of the future (a decade, perhaps two) before its time, but the handling was definitely dodgy. Straight lines were more its thing, which was probably why Hitler liked Tatras so much. Fast, high-geared and comfortable, it was the perfect car for striding across Europe, perhaps along Hitler's new autobahn. Indeed, the Führer was often to be seen inspecting the latest models at Berlin motor shows and was heard to say of the T77: 'This is a car for my roads.'

The shape of the Tatra T87 is not merely a stylist's whimsy or fashion statement, it's an exercise in sound aerodynamic theory – or 'streamlining', as it was still known in 1936. That's right, in 1936, Tatra was offering a five-seater, 100mph aerodynamic saloon.

"Indeed, the Führer was often to be seen inspecting the latest models at Berlin Motor shows and heard to say of the T77: 'This is a car for my roads.'"

A Tatra T87 shortly after killing a German officer.
Pic: Martin Buckley Archive

3

CARS OF EXCESS

If we didn't know better, we'd think that some of the celebrities featured in this chapter had made a Faustian pact at a crucial stage in their careers. In return for a Jaguar E-Type or an Aston Martin DB6, they would have to wear safari jackets, very stupid trousers and a profoundly ludicrous hairstyle for all eternity or until their career hit the holiday camp circuit.

Alternatively, as a form of punishment for transgressions in a previous existence, maybe certain celebrities were obliged to bear the mark of shame in the form of history's most horrible 'luxury cars'. We leave it to readers to judge which of the famous fall into this category, but a great many of the photographs seem to feature either beautiful cars owned by ludicrously dressed people, or ludicrous cars owned by even more ludicrously dressed people.

You could lay yourself open to criticism as an oil magnate with an artistic vision that resulted in making a coach-built Silver Wraith as appealing as a dinner date with Joseph Stalin. Or, a refreshingly tactless spouse who quite possibly aided a famous marque towards a badge-engineered twilight.

DOCKER'S DAIMLERS:
Golden Daimlers designed by Norah

The Dockers – Sir Bernard and Lady Norah – were the inspiration behind the five outrageous Daimler show cars of the 1950s: Stardust, Blue Clover, Silver Flash, the Gold Car and Golden Zebra.

Sir Bernard Docker, 53 when he met Lady Norah Collins, 43, in 1948, was managing director of

BSA, the group that owned Daimler. He was a very rich man, mainly noted for owning Britain's largest private yacht, *Shemera*. Norah later admitted it was his 'most attractive feature'.

Norah was a successful former London dance hostess at the Café de Paris who had married two millionaires within five years. Lady Docker immediately took a close interest in her husband's business affairs, becoming a director of Hoopers, exclusive coachbuilders specialising in Daimler and Rolls-Royce conversions.

Her aim in life was to raise the profile of Daimler. In her Mayfair flat, Lady Docker sketched out a massive limousine with all its brightwork finished in gold leaf.

The 'great unwashed' inspect Lady Docker's Gold Car.
Pic: Martin Buckley Archive

GUCCI'S HIDEBOUND FLOP:
No wonder the dynasty barred it

In the mid 1980s Paolo Gucci decided he wanted to build a limited edition car with matching luggage as a Gucci-branded item. The car he chose was Jaguar's XJ-S. Not just any XJ-S, mind you, but the XJ-S Eventer, the coachbuilt estate version produced by Lynx Motors of Hastings, in the south of England. A prototype was produced, brochures were printed and a car – the only car – was dispatched to design-conscious Geneva to be displayed at the motor show. That was when the trouble started. Paolo didn't have the rights to the Gucci name in Switzerland and other members of the cursed Italian fashion dynasty took exception. Lawyers became involved and the car was hurriedly de-badged and displayed as a Lynx. With its two-tone paint, electric-blue alligator leather and jewelled gear shift knob, it was certainly finished in true Gucci style, but was destined to be the only one ever built. Paolo owned it until his death, parking it at his residence near London, and it still resides somewhere in the UK with an enthusiast.

"Paolo didn't have the rights to the Gucci name in Switzerland and other members of the cursed Italian fashion dynasty took exception."

**Front cover of the brochure for the car that never was.
Pic: Lynx Motors International**

Lynx

disegno di

PAOLO 🄿🄶 GUCCI

GOLD JAGUAR:
Centre of attention at New York show

The MkII Jaguar, beloved of crooks and bank managers alike, was one of the top-selling cars imported into America. The spectacular centre-piece of Jaguar's 1960 New York motor show stand was a highly exclusive 3.8 litre MkII saloon with all its chrome-plated parts – including the wire wheels – finished in real gold. Then, a standard MkII was selling in North America for $5,000 and the estimated value of the gold MkII was $25,000. What happened to it? For that matter what happened to the Fiat 130 Coupé with gold-plated door handles that belonged to the singer Dusty Springfield? It was last spotted in unglamorous Luton, UK headquarters of Vauxhall, the General Motors offshoot.

> "When a standard MkII was selling in North America for $5,000 the estimated value of the gold MkII was $25,000."

Peter Stringfellow would have loved it: the gold-plated MkII Jaguar in New York.
Pic: Martin Buckley Archive

SULTAN'S ROLLS COLLECTION
He bought 3,000 of them (allegedly)

The Sultan of Brunei is the world's biggest Rolls/Bentley man and has, allegedly, bought more than 3,000 of them, virtually keeping the factory going at times with multi-million pound contracts to develop and build one-off specials. How about a four-wheel-drive estate version of the Continental Coupé, or a four-door saloon Continental just for smoking around in? Londoners might have caught themselves doing a double take on that one – black with heavily smoked glass – as it cruises between upmarket locations when the Sultan is in town. As a polo enthusiast the Sultan was becoming rather embarrassed by the amount of wheelspin in his standard Bentley Turbo when traversing the grass. He commissioned Bob Jankel to build a 4x4 version and also convert it into an estate. It used a Volvo four-wheel-drive system with hydraulic power to the front hubs. Jankel built 20 of the £250,000 cars, most for the Sultan.

"How about a four-wheel drive estate version of the Continental Coupé, or a four-door saloon Continental just for smoking around in?"

One of the world's least
useful estate cars.
Pic: Chelsea Workshop

Surely influenced by a certain pink Rolls-Royce driven by a wooden actor?

Pic: Frank Dale and Stepsons

FRUA'S PHANTOM FIASCO:
Probably inspired by Lady Penelope

The Phantom VI was for many years the biggest and most expensive car in the Rolls-Royce line-up, a vast limousine intended for royalty, heads of state, tycoons and the odd pop star. Most of them had traditional Park Ward bodywork reminiscent of the Silver Cloud, but in the early 1970s two chassis were released to have specialist bodywork fitted to a design by the Italian stylist Frua. Better remembered for his 60s Maseratis, Pietro Frua created a vast but elegant two-door convertible that was perhaps subliminally inspired by Lady Penelope's 'FAB 1' Rolls from the TV puppet show *Thunderbirds*. Built to the order of a Swiss customer, that car was two years in the making as the Italian designer struggled to overcome the language barrier at Rolls-Royce's plant at Crewe in England where, it seems, nobody understood Italian (or bothered to hire an interpreter). A second four-door Frua Phantom along the same lines was embarked upon in 1971 but Frua died before the project was completed and the last Frua Phantom was sold on several times to new owners before being finished.

> "Pietro Frua created a vast but elegant two-door convertible that was perhaps subliminally inspired by Lady Penelope's 'FAB 1' Rolls from the TV puppet show *Thunderbirds*."

GULBENKIAN'S UGLY ROLLERS:
Oil magnate commissioned curious limousines

Nubar Gulbenkian, an Armenian-born playboy and eccentric millionaire who lived permanently in London's posh Ritz Hotel, made his money in oil and enjoyed spending it, especially on cars. In the late 1940s he raced a chauffeur-driven Buick Super from Estoril to Sintra against an SS100 driven by the youthful arch-cad Alan Clark, a British politician (now dead) best remembered for his love life. Gulbenkian could afford to indulge his rather eccentric tastes and commissioned a series of aesthetically curious Rolls-Royce limousines. The most hideous was a Hooper creation built to Gulbenkian's requirements that emerged in 1947 on a Silver Wraith chassis. The full-width aero flow treatment of the sacred radiator grille outraged traditionalists (in fact it remained intact beneath the outer skin). Rolls-Royce were not happy about the car and Hooper was uneasy about putting its name to it, but needed the work. Gulbenkian later redeemed himself with handsome designs on the Wraith chassis.

> **"Rolls-Royce was not very happy about the car and Hooper were uneasy about putting there name to it, but needed the work."**

OBER 17, 1947
Autocar
923

Possibly the world's ugliest Rolls-
Royce, but Nulbar liked it.
Pic: Autocar

TOPLESS TVR:
Inebriated hacks meet 'Busty Bev'

It wouldn't be allowed today but, in the less politically correct 1970s, topless models (women, that is, not cars) would be a feature of TVR motor show stands on press day. Inebriated hacks, staggering under the weight of the complimentary snacks from the Datsun stand (the worst cars always had the best food) would sidle over to the TVR stand at the appointed hour. There, they would letch over 'Busty Bev' (or whoever), displaying her assets astride the bonnet of a Taimar Turbo. Such spectacles were useful to distract critics from the dated styling of the cars. Legend has it that one year a luckless young model caught her breast on a sharp windscreen wiper, lost the implant and sued TVR – but this may just be an urban myth.

"Such spectacles were useful to distract critics from the dated styling of the cars."

Cheap, vulgar and unnecessary...
the girl's quite cute though.
Pic: Martin Buckley Archive

LORD HANSON:
Made a killing with sale of one-off Bentley

A long-time Crewe customer Lord Hanson (he was ennobled in 1983), paid £14,000 to have a one-off Bentley T1 constructed by the Italian coachbuilders Pininfarina: a standard Mulliner Park Ward Shadow two-door would have cost him around £7,000.

He owned the one-off Bentley for 20 years, selling to a collector in south-east Asia at the height of the classic car boom in the 1990s when his instinct for a killing got the better of him.

'I had an American friend who was an amateur designer,' said Lord Hanson. 'He wanted a Rolls-Royce and I wanted a Bentley Continental, which I hoped would be a prototype for future Bentley Continentals. I felt if we produced something beautiful they might follow it up. In the end my friend didn't pursue his idea but I approached Sergio Pininfarina in about 1965 – I had met him before when I bought a Ferrari Superfast. He got quite excited about the idea and agreed to do it at cost price.

"He got quite excited about the idea and agreed to do it at cost price, because he felt he would be able to persuade Rolls-Royce to use his prototype as the new Bentley Continental."

The Hanson Bentley with later Shadow II
bumpers: another one for Lady Penelope.
Pic: Frank Dale and Stepsons

Possibly the coolest estate – or
shooting break – of them all.
Pic: Aston Martin Lagonda

ASTON MARTIN ESTATES:
Built for DB's country pursuits

Bill Harrah, Las Vegas casino tycoon and car collector, had a Ferrari-engined Jeep built in the mid-1960s because, well, just because he could. Even today the Sultan of Brunei likes nothing better than to have the roof of his latest Ferrari hacked off and then turned into a useful family hauler.

When business man and country gentleman David Brown had a shooting break Aston DB5 built for his own use in 1965, the idea of a desirable dual-purpose car was something quite new.

He built a dozen DB5 estate cars for himself and his landed gentry mates to use when pursuing country sports on their private estates. The story goes that in September 1965 DB called a board meeting and was accompanied by his Labrador dog. He plonked him on the boardroom table and said: 'Build me something he can sit in.' Coachbuilders Harold Radford of Hammersmith, west London, converted the cars.

The DB6 version of Astons shooting break concept was never as pretty: somehow the back end didn't lend itself to the idiom and Radford – by then part of Rolls-Royce dealer HR Owen – built only six of these cars. Three additional DB6 Breaks were constructed by Panelcraft.

A one-off DBS load hauler was built by FLM Panelcraft for a fisherman but the DB5 and six shooting breaks had no worthy immediate successor of equal gravitas.

> "He plonked his dog on the boardroom table and said 'build me something he can sit in'."

CARS OF THE STARS

What defines a star? To the authors, anyone who combines the requisite degrees of talent, dress-sense, exclusivity and individual taste in cars might find a place in this chapter. Many of the pictures are of the PR-handout genre, allowing the buyers of magazines to inwardly marvel at the lifestyles of their heroes and heroines while reacting in scandalised pleasure to their supposed excess. The elegant matching Bristols owned by Stewart Granger and Jean Simmons were in stark contrast to the powder-blue Diana Dors Cadillac Eldorado convertible. In an era when a British family car à la the Standard Eight could be sold with a 'rain and dust-sealed boot' (i.e. it doesn't open) and 'decadence' meant eating too many chocolate Bourbons, the Dors' Eldorado was proof of her outrageous lifestyle. Indeed, at the end of the 'fifties, an eminent clergyman denounced La Dors as a 'wayward hussy' although the Cadillac probably had little to do with that.

Peter Sellers bought and sold more than 100 cars between 1945 and 1980, while Elvis or Sinatra, as American icons, were expected to have a loud taste in cars. Elvis's motoring career included events that were unusual even by US-standards, from shooting his De Tomaso to having a flashing blue light and police siren fitted to his Mercedes-Benz 280SL and going out on unpaid highway patrol duties in his role as a badge-carrying county sheriff.

JIMMY TARBUCK:
Great British COM1C

Jimmy Tarbuck? What can we say: 1970s and '80s British mainstream comedy (mother-in-law jokes) and best mates with Bruce Forsyth. 'Alternative comedy is an alternative to comedy' he once said. Professional Scouser, second only to Cilla Black (one-time friend of the Beatles) but hasn't lived in Liverpool for nearly 40 years. Bernard Manning said he was 'about as funny as a burning orphanage'. ITV quiz shows. *Winner takes all* (make a twerp of yourself and win an electric kettle). Glossy photos in the *TV Times*. Quiz questions in *Look-In*. Summer variety specials filmed in sunny Bridport. Pantomime in Southsea. Dispensing chirpy Scouse humour on chat shows. Pro celebrity golf. Wasn't Mrs Thatcher wonderful. Blah, blah, blah...

Look, Jimmy Tarbuck (one-time host of TV's *Sunday Night at the London Palladium*, once ran a Silver Cloud with the registration plate COM1C.

Doesn't that say it all?

One slip and his golfing career would have been over forever. JT with that plate.
Pic: Martin Buckley Archive

OLIVER REED:
Drove under influence of bad taste

Oliver Reed bought a Panther DeVille in the late 1970s. Superficially this was the perfect transport for Reed (British actor, hell raiser and alcoholic) who once hurled bricks at a friend's Mercedes-Benz. Flamboyant Ollie liked to think of himself as a showman and the DeVille managed the rare trick of being improbably expensive while resembling a kit-car. The DeVille was fitted with BMC 'land crab' doors – the doors of doom. Some other cars fitted with these doors were rather good – the Austin Kimberley, the Wolseley 6 and the Austin 1800, which was once voted European car of the year. But these were the doors that helped lead to the demise of the British Motor Corporation. Whether this curse extended to poor Ollie, forcing him to become as ubiquitous a 1980s chat-show guest as Kenneth Williams, and to appear in Ukrainian-filmed B-movies, remains a matter for conjecture, although chronic alcoholism cannot have helped. Still it's pleasant to note that Ollie finally managed to escape the curse in *Funny Bones* and *Gladiator*, reminding his fans of all the good work he previously achieved for Joe Losey and Ken Russell.

> "Despite Ollie's deeply tedious image as a 'hell raiser' he was never once prosecuted for drunk driving."

Peter Sellers' Aston Martin DB4 was put to work in the film
The wrong arm of the law, here with Arthur Mullard as a
passenger.
Pic: Martin Buckley Archive

PETER SELLERS:
Fame brought a Cadillac Eldorado

Peter Sellers, star of films as diverse as *The Pink Panther* and *Dr Strangelove*, remains one of the celebrities most associated with the Mini. Shortly before his death he wrote the foreword to a book on the subject. In the early 1960s, readers of *Motor* or *Autocar* would be used to seeing pictures of Sellers' latest vehicle or reading, in 1959, this classified advertisement: 'Titled car wishes to dispose of owner.'

Initially, Sellers bought middle-class suburban transport like a Zephyr-Six and a Rover 105S, and many of his cars were acquired on hire purchase. Sellers had an infallible method with persistent creditors: 'I put all of their names on cards and put the cards into a hat at the end of the month. The card that I pull out is the one that I pay and if they're nasty to me, I shan't even put their names into the hat.' However, come the beginning of the '60s, he was in the six-figure income bracket and moved into the realm of luxury cars: a Bristol 406, a Bentley Park Ward Drophead, a Cadillac Eldorado Convertible and a Buick Riviera. His Aston Martin DB4 Vantage was featured in the 1962 film, *The Wrong Arm of The Law*.

> "I put all of their names on cards and put the cards into a hat at the end of the month. The card that I pull out is the one that I pay and if they're nasty to me, I shan't even put their names into the hat."

DIANA DORS:
Couldn't drive her 1931 Phantom

British cinema in the 1950s had great difficulty in creating female sex symbols, for the studios tended to slavishly copy the Hollywood model with results as incongruous as the Standard Vanguard Sportsman. Such was the Rank career of Miss Diana Fluck better known as Diana Dors.

"As the '50s progressed, the cars grew more and more lavish."

In 1950, when Dors was suffering from one of British cinema's regular crises, her husband Dennis bought her a 1931 Rolls-Royce Phantom. It cost £300, was a little moth-eaten and Diana didn't learn to drive until 1954. But the publicity was invaluable, particularly when Dors was taken to court for repayment arrears and described by the judge as 'a minor' since she was under 21. So, as the '50s progressed, and the peroxide was applied in ever-greater quantities, the cars grew more and more lavish. There was a V8 Pilot, the MkVII Jaguar (standard British film star transport), the Rolls-Royce Silver Cloud, the Delahaye (costing £2,750, noted the British tabloids) and finally the powder-blue Cadillac Eldorado.

Swindon's most famous daughter in a
car that required its own postal code.
Pic: Martin Buckley Archive

ELVIS PRESLEY:
Gold-plated hair-clippers in his Cadillac

Elvis Presley owned lots of cars as you might imagine: they included Rolls-Royces, Cadillacs (one equipped with gold-plated hair-clippers) and a BMW 507 bought while serving with the US Army in Germany (he later gave it away to actress Ursula Andress). Then there was his Continental II (a very upmarket Lincoln) and a Rolls-Royce Silver Cloud. In the 1970s he added a DeTomaso Pantera to his collection – this was a budget supercar, styled and built in Italy but powered by a reliable Ford V8 engine. Well, it was supposed to be reliable. In reality the build quality of the cars – which were marketed through Lincoln dealers in North America – was awful. One day Elvis wanted to go out for a drive in his yellow Pantera but it wouldn't start. So he shot it – several times. Until recently the car – now in a museum, and one of the most original remaining Panteras – still had the bullet hole in the door. Now the only evidence of the incident is a hole in the steering wheel.

Apparently, the car is very reliable these days.

"One day Elvis wanted to go out for a drive in his yellow Pantera but it wouldn't start. So he shot it – several times."

Elvis; Massive Lincoln
Convertible; and Gracelands.
What more can we say?
Pic: Pictorial Press

FRANK SINATRA:
Wedding gift Jaguar was in 9/11 dispute

Frank Sinatra indulged himself in specially customised cars like the Ghia L 6.4 and a Buick Riviera, modified by customiser-to-the-stars George Barris. Sinatra owned many Jaguars: a 1976 Jaguar XJ-S, which, equipped with a custom-designed sound system, was a wedding gift from Mrs Sinatra; and an XJ40 saloon, now more associated with down-at-heel bar owners and pub landlords than legendary crooners. This car was at the centre of a tug-of-war between a woman who donated it to a charity auction, and the couple who then bought it. Retired tugboat worker Michael Pakouda successfully bid $20,000 for the XJ40 in Englewood, New Jersey, in an auction to raise funds for those affected by the 9/11 terrorist attacks. But the woman who donated the car, Anna May Capelli, refused to hand over the keys. She said the $20,000 offer was the minimum price and was expecting it to sell for double that. A judge stopped the auction house from returning the car to Capelli and banned her from transferring the title to anyone else. Mr Pakouda had bought the car as a Christmas present for his wife, Angela, who is a lifelong Sinatra fan.

"...and even the XJ40 saloon now more associated with down-at-heel bar owners and pub landlords than legendary crooners."

Sinatra, still in his slim pre-toupé period, with a Buick Riviera.

Pic: Pictorial Press

Roger Moore, quiff perfectly under control, jumping behind the
wheel of a Volvo P1800 for another back-projected adventure.
Pic: Martin Buckley Archive

ROGER MOORE:
Elstree Studios' back-projected hero

Roger Moore, an English actor who included James Bond among his portrayals, was a handsome back-projected hero careering around Elstree Studios in *The Saint*. That role helped create a string of heroes including *The Baron* (featuring a Jensen CV8) and *Man in a Suitcase* (with the hero's combined Woodbine cigarette and Hillman Imp addictions).

In *The Saint*, Moore drove a Volvo and this came about because he was promised a car he could use on and off duty. Initially, he favoured a Jaguar MkX.

However Jaguar's response to a plan that would have won them millions of pounds worth of free publicity was British Motor Corporation-like in its intransigence. So Roger, on the recommendation of a policemen friend, opted for a Volvo P1800 – a car to amaze the great British public at a time when few imports from any country were to seen on their roads.

In the black & white episodes, the original 1962 Jensen-built model was supplanted by a '63 Swedish car and by the introduction of colour in 1965 (in response to the American market) Roger was driving an 1800S.

> "Jaguar's response to a plan that would have won them millions of pounds of free publicity was BMC-like in its intransigence."

FAMOUS FACEL OWNERS:
Stirling and Ringo rated the French supercar

Facel Vega had some of the most illustrious and famous owners of any car. Ava Gardner had three and ran over a policeman in Spain with one of them. Ringo Starr had a Facel II until the other Beatles persuaded him to sell it in favour of a Mercedes 600, which they thought was safer than the unruly 6.3 litre French supercar. In Britain Stirling Moss won't hear a word said against the HK500 he owned in the early 1960s and the same goes for Jackie Collins, Brian Rix and comedian Dave King. In America stars like Tony Curtis, Danny Kay and Joan Fontaine loved the car's combination of couture styling, cutting-edge luxury and robust V8 Chrysler power. Not all Facel's famous owners bought the cars new, however, so here's one you might not have heard about. After his role in *Easy Rider*, Peter Fonda would become a lasting symbol of the counter culture in the late '60s but at the beginning of the decade he looked a bit of a greasy geek who starred in such radical films as *Tammy and the doctor*. However he is massively redeemed by the fact that he owned a Facel Vega HK500.

> "Ringo Starr had a Facel II until the other Beatles persuaded him to sell it in favour of a Mercedes 600, which they thought was safer than the unruly 6.3 litre French supercar."

TOM JONES AND ENGELBERT HUMPERDINCK:
Traded in Jaguars for Silver Clouds

Jaguars are always favourites with up-and-coming stars, and by the time Tom Jones was beginning to earn some money in 1965, the S-Type was the car to have. Being a bit flash, Tom specified wires, white-walls and racing wing mirrors. Singing rival Engelbert Humperdinck (a Tom Jones clone, some said) bought himself exactly the same model, but painted gold. These days Rolls-Royce Motor Cars has an image problem because buyers see the marque as too ostentatious; Bentleys have sold in greater numbers for some years. In the '60s it was still the car to be seen in, the ultimate symbol of success, particularly for celebrities who had come up from working-class backgrounds. Tom Jones and Engelbert Humperdinck traded in their S-Type Jags for a pair of Silver Cloud IIIs. In the early '70s, Engelbert traded up to the ultimate, a Phantom VI Limousine.

When Engelbert felt drowsy behind the wheel of his **Silver Cloud** his sideburns took over the controls.
Pic: Pictorial Press

"In the '60s it was still the car to be seen in, the ultimate symbol of success, particularly for celebrities who had come up from working-class backgrounds."

MARCELLO MASTROIANNI:
Upstaged Fellini with BMW Michelotti

Heart-throb Italian actor Marcello Mastroianni was a keen car enthusiast with a particular passion for Lancias. In 1964 he bought a Lancia Flaminia Super Sport Zagato which he collected from the factory and had painted in a special shade of maroon. He'd owned several Ferraris (including a 250 GTO which he didn't much like) and bought his actress wife, Catherine Deneuve, a new Maserati Ghibli for her birthday. He shared his petrol-head passion with director Federico Fellini and in the 1960s the men would change their cars almost weekly in an attempt to outshine each other. 'Oh yes we had a kind of rivalry,' Mastroianni told an interviewer in 1990, 'he was just as bad as me, if not worse. It became absurd: I'd get a new car, so he had to get another one and so on. When we made *La Dolce Vita* I turned up at location to find him in a new Mercedes but I'd arrived in a BMW, with a special body by Michelotti. Fellini had a fit, he didn't like being upstaged. In the end we made a pact, because it was getting silly...'

> "He shared his petrol head passion with director Federico Fellini. In the '60s the men would change their cars almost every week in an attempt to outshine each other."

What else for the ultimate euro-smoothie than a
Lancia Flaminia Super Sport Zagato?
Pic: Martin Buckley Archive

Corgi model of the Saint's Jaguar XJ-S.

Pic: Corgi Classics

THE SAINT:
Returned to finally drive a Jaguar

Simon Templar (aka *The Saint*) was portrayed by Roger Moore in the 1960s and re-merged in 1977 in the form of the rather slighter Ian Ogilvy in the appropriately named *The Return of The Saint*.

Jaguar had turned down Moore's request for an E-Type but by then they were in a very different position. The company was almost smothered within the chaotic and imploding British Leyland empire, and no longer under the steady guidance of founder Sir William Lyons. Jaguar was struggling to persuade buyers that its new V12 engined XJ-S coupé was a worthy successor to the virile E-Type. They didn't need asking twice when a request from ITC appeared for an XJ-S. In fact two were used: an automatic and an ex-press demonstrator manual version (one of only a handful built). Both were fitted with sunroofs for filming purposes and both, of course, were white. Ogilvy liked the manual car so much he asked if he could drive it back to the UK after a filming session in Rome. Perhaps he was trying to reproduce *Autocar* magazine's stunt of only using top gear so as to demonstrate the V12 engine's torque. Maybe he just forgot he was in the manual. Either way he'd burned the clutch out by the time he arrived in Florence.

> "Jaguar didn't need asking twice when a request from ITC appeared for an XJ-S."

ADAM AND EVELYNE:
Matching cars for movie heart-throbs

Matching anoraks on married couples look rather sad but matching Bristols is quite another matter, especially if the supercar in question is the rare convertible 402 model (only 20 were built). British beefcake movie heart-throb Stewart Granger and his new wife, beautiful actress Jean Simmons, took delivery of the cars after they appeared opposite each other in the 1949 romantic comedy *Adam and Evelyne*. They named the Bristols after the two film characters (a move that would have delighted studio publicists). Jean was seen posing in NFP 2 for Christmas publicity pictures and Granger was instructed on the 402's controls by Tony Crook, who still heads Bristol Cars.

> "Stewart Granger and his new wife Jean Simmons took delivery of the cars after they appeared opposite each other in the 1949 romantic comedy *Adam and Evelyne* – they christened the Bristols with the same names."

Tony Crook of Bristol Cars shows Stewart Granger over the controls of his new 402 convertible.
Pic: Pictorial Press

Tony Hancock was such a rubbish driver he sent his
car everywhere by plane. The 300SL is en route to
the Cannes Film Festival but Tony still manages to
dress in "off duty 23 Railway Cuttings" mode.
Pic: Classic Cars

TONY HANCOCK:
Divorce battle over Merc 300SL Roadster

Tony Hancock, the lugubrious funnyman, possessed many talents and hobbies but driving was not one of them. Hancock did pass his driving test on the third attempt (in 1954) but rarely drove – his one-time co-writer Phillip Purser once noted that Hancock couldn't even cope with the intricacies of the electric razor. So the idea of him driving and maintaining a vehicle would clearly have been beyond 'The Lad'. However, his first wife, Cicely Romanis, was a very keen motorist and piloted Hancock in XK120s and, most famously, a Mercedes-Benz 300 Roadster. This is the car they took to Cannes to celebrate Hancock's film *The Rebel*. In October 1961, his wife was driving Hancock through Surrey when she suddenly braked to avoid some roadworks. Hancock went straight through the windscreen and suffered minor concussion plus two black eyes, which led to serious delays in the broadcast and recording of *The Blood Donor*, possibly the most popular *Hancock's half hour*.

The years between 1961 and 1968 saw a bitter divorce battle, with custody of the Roadster a major bone of contention, a very underrated film (*The Punch & Judy Man*) and two forgotten ITV series. Hancock's income remained healthy and there was a succession of expensive cars, including a Cadillac Eldorado, Mercedes-Benz 220 cabriolet and an Aston Martin Volante.

> "Hancock went straight through the windscreen and suffered minor concussion plus two black eyes, both of which meaning serious delays in the broadcast and recording of The Blood Donor."

SANDIE SHAW:
Drove barefoot along a beach

The picture shows 1960s pop singer Sandie Shaw and the Lamborghini Miura she used in one of her TV shows, driving it barefoot along a beach. It isn't known whether Sandie owned a Lambo but plenty of other celebrities have and do: somehow the words 'Peter Stringfellow' and 'white Lamborghini Countach' just go together. Jamiraquai front man Jay Kay is closely associated with the Diablo and you might remember a storage driver smashing one up, trying to drive it through width restrictors that were too narrow in Chelsea. Actor Nicholas Cage is well known for his collection of Lamborghini Miuras which includes an SVJ that once belonged to that great car enthusiast, the Shah of Iran.

In 1970 Frank Sinatra ordered a Miura. It was a special order, with metallic orange paint, shag-pile carpet and wild boar leather; Sinatra delivered the leather to the factory himself.

"Frank Sinatra ordered a Miura. It was a special order, with metallic orange paint, shag-pile carpet and wild boar leather."

History doesn't relate what car Sandie Shaw owned but we liked this shot of her on the bonnet of a Miura.
Pic: Pictorial Press

'The Quiff' Harvey with his new Wood & Pickett Mini Cooper.

Pic: Martin Buckley Archive

LAURENCE HARVEY:
'How could anyone exist without a Rolls?'

Laurence Harvey was a tall figure with a baroque quiff and RADA accent; he believed himself to be a great actor and shared this view with the press.

Hirshkeh Laruska Skikne, Lithuanian-born and South African raised, arrived at London's RADA (Royal Academy of Dramatic Art) in 1946 and set about acquiring a BBC accent and, in the long term, a Rolls-Royce.

By 1954, Harvey had graduated to a MkVII Jaguar which he kept until involved in a fatal accident in it. Laurence acquired his first chauffeur-driven Rolls-Royce, a champagne coloured Silver Wraith. The correct car was as essential to Mr Harvey as his ivory cigarette holder: 'How could anyone exist without a Rolls-Royce?,' he argued.

The Silver Wraith was soon succeeded by a fawn Bentley S which, in turn, was replaced by a Vespa scooter during the Suez oil crisis. Laurence who also owned an £11,000 Rolls-Royce Silver Cloud drophead – he was now beyond the stage of an 'ordinary' Rolls-Royce. Mr. Harvey's taste was always individual and his pink Fiat Jolly was succeeded by a Wood & Pickett Morris Cooper S Mk2.

"The correct car was as essential to Mr Harvey as his ivory cigarette holder"

Along with Dusty Springfield, Hylda Baker was
one of Britain's few celebrity Fiat 130 owners.
Pic: Andrew Roberts

CONTINUING THE FEMAIL SERIES . . .

My car—and why: Hylda Bake

MISS BAKER'S is a noticeable car : over 16ft. of silver grey Fiat 130. After 18 months there are 3,000 miles on the clock. Hylda Baker, comedienne, ear-grating star of Not On Your Nellie said, frankly her car is for status.

UNLIKE her Fiat, Miss Baker is short : 4ft. 11in. Her transport is big, shiny, smooth and all over automatic. Her two previous cars were bigger — both American.

The reason she swopped to the Fiat was that the garage man brought it round for her to see and she thought, yes, that looks very nice, thank you. Of course, there was an alteration to make. She had a sunshine roof put in.

'My mum said I was a small girl with big ideas,' said Hylda, teetering

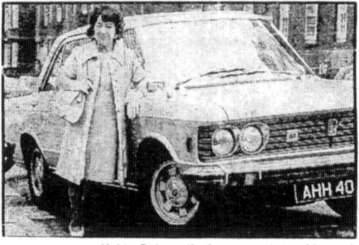

Hylda Baker : 'I always wanted a big car.'

on high heels against the glittering bonnet. She got in, sank against th sheepskin covers, which protect th transparent plastic covers, which protect the grey fabric upholstery 'while revealing its beauty'.

'I'll lower the window,' she said. 'It's all-electric.' She pressed a button and the windscreen wipers started.

Later she pressed another and the window lowered. Yet another and the radio aerial slid up. 'The sunshine roof isn't automatic,' she confessed with regret. She had considered buying an enormous car in America and bringing it over. It was all press-button, that one.

As soon as there was talk of petrol

rationing, Miss Baker whi bought a tan-coloured Mi Of course, the Fiat is mor Better for prestige. She l ONE struggling out of it

Although she appreciate value of a posh car, Hyld how to muck about with

The first vehicle she ha was an air-cooled Rover. cylinders cooled as you n drove. Cost her £25. H the crank to start it.

Fluttere

Yes, she could change and a wheel. Doesn't have one, though. Has auto change. 'It's all in th hydraulic jack . . .

'Friends advised me engine,' she said. Long, glued to green eyelid dangerously.

'I've been driving sinc No. 14. Before that I v while other people drove, thing. I always meant to something big.'

YVONNE TH

comedienne, ear-grating star of Not On Your Nellie said, frankly her car is for status.

UNLIKE her Fiat, Miss Baker is short : 4ft. 11in. Her transport

HYLDA BAKER:
Little lady with a taste for big cars

Hylda Baker is an actress and comedienne who appears so frequently on cable television that you could forget she died in 1986. As a famous variety artist, Ms Baker was her own producer, writer and director, and appeared in *Saturday Night & Sunday Morning* and *Oliver!* but *Nearest and Dearest* remains her most regularly screened legacy. True, it may now be difficult to sit through as a comedy but it remains fascinating for the performances of the underplaying Jimmy Jewell and the vibrant overplaying of Hylda Baker. *Nearest* ran for six years, plus the obligatory spin-off film, and allowed Hylda to indulge in her hobby of acquiring expensive cars.

She was a knowledgeable motorist and by the late 1950s, like many variety stars, she favoured Canadian-built 'American' cars such as her Ford Fairlane 500 Hardtop. In the 1960s she graduated to a MkX Jaguar. Though only 4ft11in, Hylda favoured large cars and was certainly able to afford them. Variety may have more or less collapsed circa 1960 but Hylda's ability as a straight actress in both the cinema and on stage, meant that by 1974 she was one of the very few British owners of a Fiat 130 saloon. A feature in the *Sunday Mirror* that year breathlessly gushes about the wonders of the Fiat's tinted glass and electric windows, which if nothing else demonstrates how distant the 1970s really are.

"She was one of the very few British owners of a Fiat 130 saloon."

'Yeah, and can you send out three large steaks
and two bottles of champagne.'
Pic: Pictorial Press

LIONEL BART:
Obsessed with car phones and gadgets

Showbiz legend Lionel Bart began his musical career by playing the washboard in a skiffle band and soon graduated to writing pop songs with Tommy Steele and Mike *Randall & Hopkirk (Deceased)* Pratt. By 1960 Lionel was earning as much as £10,000 a week from his stage shows and hit singles but by 1970 he had squandered his fortune on drink and a coterie of hangers-on. Having sold the rights to his shows he disposed of his Chelsea homes and ended up living above a shop. Cars were a brief obsession and he loved gadgets, like the radio car phone fitted to a VW Karmann Ghia.

To Mr Anglia Driver 1960, a Karmann Ghia would have been the height of exotica, its Beetle mechanics notwithstanding Also remember that mobiles were still at least 20 years away and many Britons didn't have a phone in their home, never mind their car. Bart's four cars had phones, including his most famous, a Facel Vega, the quintessential jet-setter's car.

"By 1960 Lionel was earning as much as £10,000 a week from his stage shows and hit singles but by 1970 he had squandered his fortune on drink and a coterie of hangers-on."

CHARLIE DRAKE:
Zodiac was a sign of stardom

"If you were really successful you could opt for the Zodiac Convertible, with automatic transmission to match its semi-automatic hood"

Charlie Drake bought a Ford MkII Zodiac after making the transition from children's to adult TV comedy. If you were in show business in late 1950s Britain, a new Zodiac was often the first sign you had 'made it' – it could be driven to your next headlining appearance at Butlins holiday camp in Bognor Regis and prominently parked so that all could wonder at the two-tone paint, white-wall tyres and cigarette lighter. The Zodiac could appeal to young businessmen and rock'n'roll stars alike, from Brian Epstein, whose swish car impressed the Beatles on their first meeting in 1961 to the be-quiffed British Elvis clones who all wanted to be all-round entertainers. If you were really successful you could opt for the Zodiac Convertible, with automatic transmission to match its semi-automatic hood, and if you wanted to chase Jaguars on the new M1, you could specify overdrive, and work your way through five column-mounted gear-speeds. Later, Charlie Drake moved up to the glamour of a Facel Vega but, because he was too short to see over the wheel properly, he kept knocking down fence posts in the New Forest where he lived.

Charlie Drake lives the 1950s dream in his two-tone Ford Zodiac.

Pic: Pictorial Press

5 CRIMES & MISDEMEANOURS

Apologies in advance to anyone expecting pursuit stories of the 'MkII Jaguar pursued by black police Wolseley 6/110 at Hatton Garden' variety. We did include The Great Train Robbery, if only to dispel illusions created by that great film Robbery, as the main getaway vehicles were Land Rovers.

We've tended to select cars that have become indelibly associated with crimes of various descriptions, and not all of them particularly exotic models. In addition to the stories behind Stephen Ward's XK150 or Aldo Moro's Fiat 130 Berlina, you will read about Ford of Argentina's long-running Falcon model that, by the 1970s, had become synonymous with some of the worst human rights abuse of the late 20th century.

In fact Fords, through no fault of Dearborn, seem to come off rather badly in this chapter, from OJ Simpson's Bronco ride to the Ford Corsair used by Lord Lucan (surely one of the most banal cars to ever feature in a high-profile murder case).

However, to prove our lack of Ford-bias, there are also the tales of a certain peer of the realm, an insurance company and an awful lot of Ferraris, a Fiat and a runaway British army tank, which really should have been made into an episode of The Persuaders.

GREAT TRAIN ROBBERS:
Chose Austin lorry
instead of Jaguars

Originally, it had been suggested that MkII Jaguars, with their rear seats removed, should be used by the Great Train Robbers to transport the mailbags to their hideout. Ironically, compact Jaguars without a rear seat were also favoured by police in many parts of the UK in the 1960s. However, in the end the felons used an ex-army Austin lorry along with two Land Rovers in the aftermath of Britain's most legendary modern crime. The vehicles, stolen from central London, had identical registration plates (BMG 757A) to confuse the police. The Land Rovers were discovered at the gang's hideout at Leatherslade Farm in Buckinghamshire. One is now owned by a private collector.

The Great Train Robbers used identical number plates to keep the police guessing.
Pic: Martin Buckley archive

LORD LUCAN:
He made the Ford Corsair famous

The Corsair's association with the 1974 Lucan murder case is probably the only thing most people can remember about this most forgettable of Fords. Although he owned a Mercedes, Lucan borrowed the dark-blue 1966 Corsair from friend Michael Stoop several days before he allegedly killed his children's nanny, Sandra Rivett, in the belief it was his estranged wife Veronica, in the basement of their London Belgravia house. The car was found later covered inside in bloodstains in the English Channel port of Newhaven. In the Corsair's boot was the most damning piece of evidence against Lucan – a 16-inch piece of lead pipe bound with surgical tape that was identical to the weapon that had been used to murder Rivett. Richard John Bingham, the 7th Earl of Lucan, was never traced.

> **"In the Corsair's boot was the most damning piece of evidence against Lucan – a sixteen inch long piece of lead pipe bound with surgical tape that was identical to the weapon that had been used to murder Rivett."**

The Lucan affair was one of the Corsair's very few moments in the limelight as the grizzly get-away car. On the brighter side, celebrity Corsair owners include Joyce Grenfell and actor David Lodge.
Pic: Ford Motor Company

Corsair- the car that's seen but not heard

Smooth, silent V-Power Simply turn the ignition key in your new Corsair V4 and you have started a quiet revolution. No matter whether you're driving through early morning streets, or sharing the road with everyone else in town, the Corsair goes about its business quietly and smoothly. Very smoothly. Corsair's fine engineering means smooth acceleration, all-synchromesh gears mean smooth changing. Crossflow-heads and bowl-in-piston combustion chambers mean smooth performance. Front disc brakes mean smooth stopping.

But V-engine efficiency isn't the whole story Instruments, controls, interior trim and upholstery all add up to one of the most distinctively stylish cars on the road. And with *Aeroflow* ventilation the air inside is as fresh as the looks outside. And if all this isn't enough, there is an even more powerful, more stylish GT version that can get up and go to 60 mph in 14 seconds. Or there's the latest newcomer to the Corsair Range—the Corsair V4 GT Estate Car combining the elegance of the Corsair with the urgency of the GT. Visit your nearest Ford Dealer and test drive a Corsair V4. The recommended delivered price is only £803 tax paid, £928 for the Corsair V4 GT. The Corsair GT Estate Car costs £1149 tax paid. *FoMoCo accessories (as illustrated) include fog and long range spot lamps, overriders, wing mirrors, radio.*

A big **V6** Fiat, like the one the former Italian premier
was being driven in on the day of his kidnapping.
Pic: Martin Buckley Archive

MURDER OF ALDO MORO:
Kidnapped from Fiat 130

A dark-blue Fiat 130 carrying Aldo Moro, the former Italian premier and leader of the Christian Democratic Party, was being driven towards the parliamentary compound on the morning of March 16, 1978. It was closely followed by three security guards in a white Alfa Romeo. As the small convoy approached a road junction, a large saloon bearing diplomatic licence plates suddenly overtook the Alfa and the Fiat, stopping so suddenly at the junction that the Alfa cannoned into the back of the 130. The driver and the passenger of the big saloon then walked towards the Fiat and shot dead the chauffeur and the bodyguard in the front passenger seat. At that moment four men in Alitalia uniforms, who had been standing at the junction as though waiting for a bus, walked over to the 130 and produced semi-automatic weapons from their flight bags, killing all three occupants of the Alfa Romeo. The team from the Red Brigade then kidnapped Moro in an attempt to engineer the release of 13 Brigade members standing trial in Turin. When the Italian government refused to accede to their demands, the terrorists murdered Moro on May 9, 1978. It is an event still vividly remembered in Italian society.

> "As the small convoy was approaching a road junction, a large saloon bearing diplomatic licence plates suddenly overtook the Alfa and the Fiat, stopping so suddenly at the junction that the Alfa cannoned into the back of the 130."

Stephen Ward loved his Jaguar XK150 drophead; here he's played by John Hurt in *Scandal*, a movie about the Profumo Affair.

Pic: Pictorial Press

STEPHEN WARD:
Drove his XK150 to visit shebeens

Dr. Stephen Ward was best remembered for his part in the Profumo Affair: government minister, Soviet attache, call girls etc.

Born in 1912, Ward held an American doctorate in osteopathy and by the 1950s seemed to have established himself as a bon viveur with a Harley Street practice, smart London apartment equipped with two-way mirrors and connections with the aristocracy. Ward and his chums also enjoyed cruising the streets of Notting Hill in his 1959 white Jaguar XK150 and visiting West Indian shebeens (unlicensed houses selling liquor). But by 1963, Ward was abandoned by his influential society friends and found himself at the Old Bailey on a very dubious charge of 'living off immoral earnings'. Ward took a fatal overdose and in his suicide note remarked: 'The car needs oil in the gearbox by the way. Be happy in it'.

> "Ward and his chums also enjoyed cruising the streets of Notting Hill in his 1959 white XK150 and visiting West Indian shebeens."

LORD BROCKET'S SCAM:
He claimed insurance on chopped-up Ferraris

Lord Brocket promoted himself as a 'passionate' Italian car enthusiast in the hyped-up classic car market of the late 1980s. Then he ran into trouble with Customs and Excise officials over misrepresentation of Ferrari values and suspicion was arroused when five cars and four engines were reported stolen from his estate north of London in 1991. General Accident, his insurers, could not understand how the three '50s Ferraris and a Maserati Birdcage could have been removed from the high-security Brocket Hall which hosted VIP conferences. GA refused to pay the £4.6 million claim and Brocket began legal proceedings. In 1994 the action was settled out of court with both sides paying their own costs. In 1995, the cars and parts were found, chopped-up and sunk in oil drums in a North London lock-up.

> "Then in the spring of 1995 the remains of the cars and parts were found, chopped-up and sunk in oil drums in a north London lock-up."

Brocket was charged with attempted deception and two former employees told a court how they cut the cars up with an angle grinder – assisted by Lord Brocket – and burned the parts in the boiler house of the stately home. In February 1996, Brocket was sent to prison for five years.

The Brocket Ferraris in happier days – tucked-
up in his lordship's heated motor house.
Pic: Classic Cars

Steve McQueen with his
favourite toy, the Jaguar XK-SS.
Pic: Pictorial Press

STEVE MCQUEEN:
Collected 37 speeding tickets in his Merc

As well as being a gifted actor, Steve McQueen could drive pretty well, and when he began to earn real money in the early 1960s, he could indulge his passion for fast cars. He wasn't one for vast, vulgar collections but preferred to keep a few choice jewels like a Ferrari Lusso, a Porsche or two, American rarities like a 'step-down' Hudson Hornet and his much loved Jaguar XK-SS, which McQueen raced up and down the roads annoying his movie-star neighbours. When filming *The Great Escape* in Germany in 1962, McQueen bought a Mercedes 300SL which he drove to the studio at high speed every day, usually with the local police in hot pursuit. During the course of the filming he collected 37 speeding tickets, about one fine every three days. When he failed to show his driving licence he was almost jailed. In the end he crashed the Mercedes into a tree, leaving the film company to stump up for the repairs to the scenery.

"During the course of the filming he collected 37 speeding tickets, about one fine every three days."

NOBLE FAILURES, MISSED OPPORTUNITIES

In an episode of The Simpsons entitled O Brother Where Art Thou? Homer is given a chance to design his own dream car. Unfortunately, its premiere is greeted with a level of appalled silence reminiscent of two British car launch parties – the Austin 3-Litre in 1967 and the Lea Francis Lynx in 1960.

This is the chapter for all such quixotic automotive efforts and missed opportunities but we veer towards the less charted failures. Cars such as the Austin 3-Litre and the Madrid taxi driver's favourite, the Anglo-American-Franco-Spanish Chrysler 2-litre, are just too mediocre to be considered and countless thousands of words have been written about the Edsel. The same applies to the Allegro, Maxi and Marina, that are all currently popular in a post-modern ironic way with those who find hilarity in the collapse of an entire industry. All three of BL's finest could all be considered lost opportunities – yes, even the Marina - but we preferred to concentrate on BMC's two major 1964 models as they represented a watershed for Europe's then largest motor manufacturer.

ROVER P6BS:
Killed-off as threat to E-Type

The annals of post-war British motoring history are full of intriguing what-ifs and might-have-beens, none more so than the Rover P6BS. Created as an after-hours pet project by Rover designers in the mid-1960s it was a fast and wieldy mid-engined coupé that would have performed as well as an E-Type Jaguar, handled rather better and cost several hundred pounds less. And that was its downfall. When Rover joined forces with Jaguar, Triumph and then BMC to form British Leyland, the BS was suddenly an in-house threat to the Jaguar. Sir William Lyons, the boss of Jaguar, is reputed to have insisted that the BS project be killed off for this reason. Rover engineers were sufficiently confident in the car that it was released for a full road test to *Motor* magazine. It received a glowing report but no reprieve was granted and today, more than three decades on, the car languishes in a corner at the British Motor Heritage Museum.

Rover's promising mid-engined BS Coupé, sadly one of many casualties of the new BLMC
Pic: Martin Buckley Archive

PININFARINA BMC 1800:
Showed how the 'land crab' could have been

The British motor industry… where did it all go wrong? I blame Alec Issigonis, designer of the 1959 Mini. I reckon that like all good heroes, he was fatally flawed. Management invested too much faith in the ideas of Issigonis. They didn't grasp that his high-minded concepts of engineering purity (maximum space, minimum size), would never work on anything bigger than an 1100 (sold separately as an Austin and a Morris). Issigonis was a two-hit wonder, with the Mini and Morris Minor, and should have been given a gold clock and a generous pension sometime in the early 1960s.

"That svelte CX-like body would have put BMC years ahead of the game."

Instead they let him design the 1800 (sold as a Wolseley, as well as Austin and Morris). This is perhaps the most sterile and unsexy car ever devised (rightly nicknamed 'land crab') and a crucial player in what we'd now regard as the big volume Ford Mondeo/Vauxhall Vectra part of the UK market.

A few buyers may have been impressed by the interior space but few needed it. Fewer would have known, or cared, about the immense stiffness inherent in its bodyshell.

Did the fortunes of BL pivot on this car? Pininfarina's
elegant **BMC 1800** proposal that would have finally
dispensed with the unsexiest car ever.
Pic: Martin Buckley Archive

Comical styling of the disastrous Leaf Lynx.

Pic: Classic Cars

LEA FRANCIS LEAF LYNX:
Comedian designed car that changed colour under the show lights

The bizarre Lea Francis roadster was a last ditch attempt by an old-established English sports car maker based in Coventry to build a car to revitalise the company. Lea Francis had been surviving since the mid-1950s on government subcontract work but, as this dried up towards the end of the decade, it became imperative to re-establish the marque. Enter, at the 1960 Earls Court London motor show, the Leaf Lynx. Powered by a Ford Zephyr engine that alienated followers of the marque, the shape succeeded in repelling everyone else. Bulbous and cigar-like, with side panels that anticipated the MkX Jaguar combined with a tasteful 'dustbin lid' radiator grille, the Lynx was the work of a comedian and part-time stand-up comic called Arthur Keene who, as a day job, did publicity and styling for the company. Roy Brown of Ford was reckoned to be a pretty fair crooner – but the Lynx's cause was not helped by the fact that the trendy 'Royal Purple' paint, under the Earls Court lights, turned the colour of what one observer called 'ferret droppings'. Not one single order was taken at the show and the marque died, although several ill-conceived attempts have been made to revive it more recently.

> "The Lynx was the work of a comedian and part time stand-up comic called Arthur Keene who, as a day job, did publicity and styling for the company."

FACEL LE MANS CAR:
Patron said it was 'stolen by gangsters'

Shortly before Facel closed its doors as a motor manufacturer its patron, Jean Daninos, was hatching a plan to build a Le Mans car. It was to be a mid-engined car with a 500bhp Chrysler engine, a Colotti gearbox and Dunlop discs. The tubular frame and the body – judging by the side-profile drawing which seems to be the only picture that exists of the car – looked remarkably like a GT40. Daninos had rented Zandvoort for testing but called the project off when it looked as though Facel was about to go under. A prototype was almost completed but according to Daninos was 'stolen by gangsters', although not before most of the running gear was sent back to its suppliers. Rumour has it that the remains of the car still exist somewhere in France.

"A prototype was almost completed but according to Daninos was stolen by gangsters."

This line drawing is all that remains of the intriguing Facel Vega racer.
Or is it...?
Pic: Martin Buckley archive

Peter Monteverdi looks pleased with his
Monteverdi Sierra, based on a Plymouth.
Pic: Martin Buckley Archive

PETER MONTEVERDI:
Sought revenge against Enzo Ferrari

For 40 years Peter Monteverdi, descendant of the 17th-century composer, was Switzerland's only player in the world motor industry.

His first cars – called MBM – were Formula Junior racers but he was also Switzerland's first Ferrari dealer. Sadly the decade-old agency ended badly in 1964 when Monteverdi refused to pay upfront for a consignment of 100 cars. Enzo Ferrari found another importer but made an enemy in the short-tempered Monteverdi, who decided to get revenge by building his own supercar.

Enter, at the 1967 Frankfurt show, the Monteverdi 375S with a svelte body styled by Frua and powered by a 7.2 litre Chrysler engine. For the next eight years this model spawned a whole raft of pricey GT cars, associated with the rich, the powerful and Gerald Harper in the British TV series, *Hadleigh*.

From 1970, he built a 145mph limousine version and the King of Qatar still runs five of them on the palace fleet. The Swiss government preferred to drive Mercedes, even when Monteverdi offered them a free car.

"Enzo found another importer but made an enemy in the short-tempered Monteverdi, who decided to get revenge by building his own supercar."

SIR JOHN WHITMORE:
Stopped from sorting out the 'Flying Pig'

Just before Ford launched its massive Ford Zephyr/Zodiac MkIV range in April 1966, it gave gentleman racer Sir John Whitmore – noted campaigner of the Lotus Cortina in saloon racing – a prototype to test. He was appalled by the car's handling: 'It lurched and wallowed and if you went quickly over a humpback bridge the rear suspension just folded up underneath you.'

"It lurched and wallowed and if you went quickly over a humpback bridge the rear suspension just folded up underneath you."

John was a Ford dealer when the Zephyr/Zodiac MkIV 'Flying Pig' came out and wasn't surprised when the cars proved difficult to sell. 'We had them stood in fields rotting… people didn't like the size… and they were so ugly.' he said. Along with Alan Mann, who owned the GT40s John raced, Whitmore decided to sort out the handling of the car. Ford didn't want an outside engineer showing up its engineering department. Whitmore's misgivings about the MkIV were eventually vindicated because it was one of the great Ford sales disasters of the 1960s. But it starred in British TV series *Z-Cars*, *Softly Softly* and *Randall & Hopkirk (Deceased)*.

A Honda 1300 not understeering.

Pic: Martin Buckley Archive

HONDA 1300:
Air-cooled cock-up by the Supreme Advisor

The 1300 is Honda's Ford Edsel, its very own Titanic, an innocuous little car that caused a boardroom bust-up, near mutiny among the company's engineers and radically affected the influence of Mr Honda himself. After the 1300 things were never quite the same at Honda.

Soichiro Honda had a thing about air-cooling: fair enough you might say for a man who had built up a huge company making motorcycles and pint-sized city cars. But when the time came, in the mid-1960s, to design a family-sized saloon he was still pressing for air-cooling, much against the better judgement of his engineering staff who were worried the new engine might not meet future American emissions legislation.

"Buyers recognised a lemon and soon Honda was haemorrhaging money."

But Mr Honda was having none of it and the 1300 arrived in April 1969. The 1300 didn't rattle like a Beetle and developed 96bhp at 7200rpm – which made it the most powerful 1300cc mass-production saloon on the planet. Technicians loved it, drivers didn't. It was fast in a straight line – 110mph – but lost the plot through corners. Buyers recognised a lemon and soon Honda was haemorrhaging money.

A strange choice of car for a Lulu, then a teenage star.

Pic: Pictorial Press

VANDEN PLAS 4-LITRE R:
BMC stockpiled poor man's Roller

"Leonard Lord had to remove the 'BMC 1' licence plate from his own R as he was prone to being approached by irate VDP owners."

Launched in 1964, the Vanden Plas 4 litre R was the only fruit of a short-lived liaison between Rolls-Royce and the British Motor Corporation.

The high-specification wood and leather luxury saloon based on the 3-litre A110 Westminster shell had a 4-litre Rolls-Royce straight-six engine. Inside the 4-litre R had the full Vanden Plas treatment with Connolly leather on the seats and lavish walnut veneer on the dashboard, door cappings and picnic tables.

With a claimed 175bhp (gross) the smooth all-alloy seven-bearing Rolls-Royce straight-six gave the 4-litre R an impressive turn of speed. It accelerated cleanly up to the ton and road testers managed 112mph flat-out. The pretentious 4-litre R was fast and plush but no Rolls-Royce. The handling was awful, its reliability suspect and the Wolseley 6/110 offered much the same package for £900 less.

One thing was very Rolls-like – the 12mpg thirst – and BMC stockpiled hundreds of the unwanted cars in a field. They even gave them to junior salesmen who would normally be driving a humble Cambridge.

The fuel crisis killed off the beautiful Monica supercar.

Pic: Martin Buckley Archive

MONICA:
35 were built – and 25 were prototypes

The elegant Monica – named after the wife of its patron, the business tycoon Jean Tastevin – was a victim of protracted development and poor timing. Tastevin, the French railway goods-wagon builder, dreamed of creating his own grand touring car cast in the mould of the defunct Facel Vega and hired British engineer Chris Lawrence to design and develop it. The project began in the mid-1960s and was originally to have used Ted Martin's prototype 3-litre V8 but worries about the reliability of this race-bred engine – and its compatibility with automatic transmission – led to the adoption of Chrysler's V8 at the last minute. Tastevin insisted on bizarre electrically assisted locks that sounded great until the battery went flat and there was no way of getting in – or out – of the car.

"Tastevin insisted on a bizarre system of electrically assisted locks which sounded great until the battery went flat and there was now way of getting in – or out – of the car."

The body was redrawn several times – becoming both lower and wider – until the final shape was agreed. But the agonies of the development process delayed the launch of the definitive car until the 1973 Geneva motor show. The '70s Middle East fuel crisis began to make itself felt and the 150mph, £14,000 13mpg Monica was bad news. Production finished after 35 cars and 25 were prototypes.

DAIMLER MKX:
Canned because it embarrassed Jaguar

With a 220bhp V8, the Daimler MkX was faster than the Jaguar equivalent. When Jaguar acquired Daimler in 1960 it inherited the Majestic Major powered by an impressive 220bhp 4.5 litre hemi-head V8. Badge engineering was all the rage in the '60s and having successfully grafted the smaller 2.5 litre V8 into the MkII Jaguar fitting its bigger relative into the huge MkX Jaguar seemed an obvious move. This produced quite a hot-rod. In fact the Daimler MkX was embarrassingly faster than the XK-engined Jaguar with a top speed of 135mph, and to protect Jaguar's prestige, the project was canned. In any case there was a new V12 Jaguar engine on the way that was already being tested, in four-cam form, in the MkX. According to Paul Skilleter's book *Jaguar saloon cars* the prototype was so rapid during testing that its full suspension travel was taken up, allowing the tyres to touch the front wings and burn the paint off.

"The prototype circulated MIRA so rapidly that its full suspension travel was taken up, allowing the tyres to touch the front wings and burn the paint off."

**With the Daimler V8, Jaguar's big MkX was
probably a better car. So Lyons killed it.
Pic: Martin Buckley Archive**

The big Humbers were a favourite with cabinet
ministers. V8 power would have prolonged the car's life.
Pic: Martin Buckley Archive

HUMBER SC-1:
Chrysler killed off British ministerial car

Humbers were the favoured British ministerial cars of the 1950s and most of the '60s and prime minister Harold Wilson used a Humber Imperial with bomb proofing and air conditioning.

They were popular as chauffeur-driven cars and would often be featured wafting minor American celebrities about. British entertainer Jimmy Saville had one, as did the controversial Liberal Party leader Jeremy Thorpe.

In search of more power for its big 3-litre, six-cylinder Snipe and Imperial Humber saloons, Rootes turned to American V8 power in the form of Chrysler's 5.1 litre '318' engine. Unlike the Sunbeam Tiger – whose Ford V8 was a real squeeze under the bonnet of the Alpine – the Chrysler engine fitted straight in and gave the car dramatically improved 125mph performance but with a hefty fuel consumption penalty. Six SC-1 prototypes were built but Chrysler, which took over Rootes in 1967, decided to drop the big Humbers. Only one prototype survives.

"Unlike the Sunbeam Tiger – whose Ford V8 was a real squeeze under the bonnet of the Alpine – the Chrysler engine fitted straight in and gave the car dramatically improved 125mph performance."

MINI 9X:
Died so the Marina could live

In the rosy glow of nostalgia that surrounds the original Mini it is easy to forget that by the late 1960s it was looking dated and would soon be overwhelmed by a whole raft of European superminis like the Fiat 127 and Renault 5. Certainly the 9X, conceived by Alec Issigonis in 1968, could have fought the foreign competition on every front. Here was a car that was lighter than his original Mini, no larger on the outside yet offering more interior room. Weight was pared-down by the ditching of the heavy Mini sub-frames in favour of new strut and trailing arm suspension and the new overhead cam engine was much more refined and powerful. Pininfarina was hired to do a modern, glassy body with hatchback rear door. In 1968 the car was ready for production but BMC executive Donald Stokes channelled the money into the development of what he saw as a much more important machine. That was the Marina, hardly one of the design success stories of the British motor industry.

"Here was a car that was lighter than the original Mini, no larger on the outside yet offering more interior room."

Issigonis was out of favour with the Leyland bosses by the time
his carefully thought-out 9X supermini was coming to fruition.
Pic: Classic Cars

ALFA GIULIA ESTATE:
Favoured by Italian police and army

Carrozzeria Colli, coachbuilders in Milan between 1932 and 1973, will be best remembered for Giulia Super estate cars produced in the mid-1960s. Just 16 were built: the majority for the Italian police and army. The remaining cars were used as service barges by European Alfa dealer team racers in Belgium, France and, of course, Italy who at that time were campaigning GTA and GT AMs. Most of the 16 had their rear side windows panelled in and all had folding rear seats and a proper lift-up tailgate. Most used stock running gear – a 1600cc twin cam engine with a five-speed gearbox – but at least one had the lustier 1750 engine and bigger brakes from the V8-engined Montreal coupé.

"Two right-hand-drives went to UK to be used by dealers. One is currently being restored for a Japanese estate car collector but the other has long since been destroyed."

Two right-hand-drives went to the UK to be used by dealers. One is being restored by a collector who runs an estate car museum in Japan but the other has long since been destroyed. There was a factory Alfasud estate car in the '70s but there would be no Europe-wide Alfa estate until the 33 in the '80s.

The estate version of Alfa Giulia was better looking than the saloon.
Pic: Martin Buckley Archive

POVERTY FORDS:
One-speed wipers and cardboard door trim

In base-model world the trim was always vinyl, the carpets thin and the engine a little smaller than it should have been, connected to a gearbox with too few speeds. It's a world of stark-painted metal finishes, blanked-off switches, single carburettors, seats that don't recline, wind-down windows and a clock where you expected to find a rev-counter.

Stripped of their trim, poverty models were built for no-frills motoring and sold as company vehicles. It's a genre that has thrown up cars that have become almost mythical because they are so rare, like the Ford Anglia 103G with a single-speed wiper, chrome only on the grille and no trafficators. It was a car so basic that almost all have been up-rated.

BMC built an ultra-basic version of its big Austin Westminster saloon mainly for use as a police patrol car, with flat cardboard door trims and acres of painted metal.

More recently the Ford Sierra three-door was known simply as the Sierra saloon. The brochure copywriters struggled to make a virtue out of its exciting push-button radio, three-speed heater fan and concealed seat belts.

"The brochure copywriters struggled to make a virtue out of its exciting push-button radio, three-speed heater fan and concealed seat belts."

Now dumped in a lay-by near you; the 'poverty' Sierra.
Pic: Ford Motor Company

EMBARRASSING MOMENTS, DODGY DEALS

One day in the distant future historians will ponder why so many early 21st century Britons were obsessed with the minutiae of celebrities. However, any reader expecting soap opera stars will be sorely disappointed and another category of 'celebrity' lacking in this chapter is that of the British footballer – once you've read about one 19-year-old who habitually crashes Ferraris outside a nightclub, you've read them all.

Instead we've chosen to include figures of real achievement whose relationship with the car ranges from the surreal to the embarrassing. Ms. Fanny Craddock's fame lies with her refreshing approach to television cookery and aiming her Rolls -Royce at uniformed police officers. Then there is Michael Caine who, despite the fact that his best films are so associated with various types of British car didn't pass his driving test until he was nearly 50. Sometimes the cars are embarrassing: like the Aston supercar that wouldn't start at the vital moment.

TAVISTOCK LAGONDA:
Failed under the glare of the media spotlight

When Aston Martin displayed William Towns' dramatically designed Lagonda saloon at the 1976 London motor show, it took enough orders to pull the company from the brink of bankruptcy. Lord and Lady Tavistock of Woburn Abbey were old friends of Aston's new boss, Peter Sprague, and took delivery of the first production car on April 29, 1978, in full glare of the media spotlight. It was an

The Tavistock Lagonda out to grass at Woburn Abbey.
Pic: Aston Martin Lagonda

embarrassing day for all concerned. The futuristic £30,000 saloon featured an ambitious electronics system – a trendy digital dashboard and touch-sensitive controls – that nobody had mastered and the car suffered total electrical failure on the day of the grand handover at Woburn. Luckily for Aston, which had to go away and redesign the system, the Tavistocks showed great understanding.

A still from *The Italian job* with Caine and co-star.

Pic: Pictorial Press

MICHAEL CAINE:
Couldn't drive until well over 40...

Michael Caine was the star of perhaps the ultimate petrol-head film of all time, *The Italian job*. He also put the humble MkII Ford Cortina to good use in British films, be it in saving the world in *The Billion Dollar Brain* or England's menacing north-east in *Get Carter*. Late 1960s film magazines always seemed to contain pictures of Michael in his latest Rolls-Royce. Strange then that he couldn't drive.

In *Alfie* we see him behind the wheel of a Rolls-Royce Silver Cloud but Mr Caine is being towed. He didn't get a licence until the mid '70s after he moved to Los Angeles, as he explains in his autobiography, *What's it all about?* Not only is public transport almost non-existent in LA but, much more importantly to a multi-millionaire actor who could be chauffeured anywhere he wanted, shop assistants asked for your driving licence number in shops when paying by credit card and became suspicious if you could not provide it. Caine was well over 40 when he passed his test (not many people know that...) and was then able to enjoy driving his new Rolls-Royce Silver Shadow. And go shopping in LA.

> **"Caine passed his test after just a few lessons and was able to enjoy driving his brand new Rolls-Royce Silver Shadow."**

Fanny and Johnny admire their Rolls-Royce Silver Dawn.
Pic: Pictorial Press

FANNY CRADDOCK:
She cooked better than she drove

Imagine you're a socially insecure but up-and-coming advertising copywriter in Britain circa 1965. You may think your place in polite society is secure with your green and ivory Triumph 2000 in the drive of your executive home and your wardrobe of Hepworth suits, but secretly your knowledge of haute cuisine is sadly lacking. Fortunately BBC TV is on hand to help with an apparently soused Old Harrovian being bullied by a terrifying matriarch who sports the brand of cut-glass accent usually employed by renegade colonials.

Two incidents seem to help sustain her mystique, the first a motoring escapade in the 1970s. As Ms Craddock's TV career declined – colour TV revealed that all of her creations appeared to be lime green – the driving of her Silver Shadow became more and more erratic. Fanny would blithely cannon into parked cars and once aimed her Rolls-Royce at a uniformed policeman who tried to flag her down for bad driving. 'Uniformed delinquent' was Ms Craddock's opinion on the matter.

> "Fanny would blithely cannon into parked cars and, on one amazing occasion in 1972, aimed her Rolls-Royce at a uniformed policeman."

JOHN LENNON:
Bought the second ISO Fidia

John Lennon's most famous car is the psychedelic Rolls-Royce Phantom V but he had many others, including a white Mercedes 600 (George and Ringo also owned 600s). Lennon appreciated fine cars and bought various customised Radford Minis, at least one Ferrari and an ISO Fidia, a rare four-door Italian super saloon he spotted at the Earls Court London motor show in 1967. ISO has long since died but had quite a celebrity following in the '60s; Dan Blocker from Bonanza, Sonny and Cher, Lord Lucan, Pete Townshend of The Who and Lord Lichfield all owned them. Lennon's car, delivered at the end of 1967, was the second built. The Beatle, who only learned to drive in 1965, was a short-sighted driver. His most famous car-related incident happened at the wheel of an Austin Maxi. On July 1, 1969, John, Yoko, Julian and Yoko's daughter Kyoko were motoring around northern Scotland on holiday. After visiting John's aunt in Sutherland, they were involved in a serious car crash. The family was taken to hospital, where John required 17 stitches for a facial wound, Yoko 14 stitches and Kyoko four. Julian was treated for shock.

> "Despite his appreciation of fine cars Lennon – who only learned to drive in 1965 – was a short-sighted driver."

What does this switch do...? Lennon takes a squint at the ISO's impressive dashboard.
Pic: Pictorial Press

SID JAMES:
Delayed by carry on with cabby

Sid James, the star of many *Carry On* movies and Tony Hancock's sidekick on TV and radio, was from an era when all male show business stars delighted in off-duty cardigans. James' best-remembered car was an Austin FX3, for he was one of the select band of actors in British cinema who seemed to belong behind the wheel of a London black cab. In the early 1960s, he could be seen in an FX3 in *Carry On Cabby*, a Winchester in his BBC TV series *Taxi!* and finally an FX4 in the all-colour Joe Brown/Una Stubbs song-and-dance extravaganza that was *Three Hats for Lisa*. So it is entirely fitting that one of the earliest Sid-related motoring stories concerns a London cab. As the tale goes, Sid was in a cab en route to a Hancock recording session when the driver carved up a bubble car driven by an Hasidic Jew. Said the cabby to Sid: 'I hate Jews,' to which Sid's succinct reply was: 'Stop the car'. The net result of this contretemps was the cabby's head bouncing off one of the front mudguards and dislodging a headlamp, thereby delaying Sid's arrival at the BBC.

Sid James and son enjoy a moment in 1950s suburbia.
Pic: Pictorial Press

"James' best-remembered car was an Austin FX3, for he was one of the select band of actors in British cinema who seemed to belong behind the wheel of a London black cab"

LARRY PARNES:
Made singer pay for car 'present'

Popular myth still has it that Larry Parnes, a former dress-shop owner and theatrical producer, 'discovered' many pioneer British rock 'n' roll stars of the pre-Beatles era. He also managed to turn down both the Beatles and Kris Kristofferson, but in the black and white era just prior to Brian Epstein and Merseybeat, Parnes was highly newsworthy.

The national press ran a picture of three members of the Parnes stable posing with their new cars and, in 1960, Joe Brown's Ford Zephyr Mk 2 convertible, Billy Fury's MGA coupé and Vince Eager's Triumph Herald coupé must have seemed the height of decadence. The Herald was in fact a present from Parnes to Vince on his 19th birthday. Vince was driving a car that would have represented more than an average year's wage in 1960. What could go wrong?

Two weeks later Eager learned that he had in fact paid for his own present. Just to make matters worse, his Herald had been rammed by a Jowett Javelin.

> "He also managed to turn down both the Beatles and Kris Kristofferson."

A scene from an early **1960s** musical *Play it Cool*; Billy Fury (driving) plays Billy Universe. The car is a Daimler DB18. Pic: Pictorial Press

TONY CURTIS:
Reduced to sleeping in his Trans-Am

Tony Curtis was always deeply into his cars. In his time he owned a Mercedes 300SL Gullwing, Facel Vega, an Alvis and a Jensen to name just a few. He used a Ferrari Dino 206 in *The Persuaders*, a TV series of the early 1970s. Less than a decade later his career was on the skids. Strung out on cocaine and booze, he had taken to sleeping in the back seat of his silver Pontiac Trans-Am, getting respite from his marriage and work problems. He said: 'I was curled up under a blanket so nobody could see me and I could get a few hours sleep'...
The great Tony Curtis spent a lot of nights that way, sleeping in parking lots or travelling to places like Las Vegas, just to get away for a while.'

"Strung out on cocaine and booze, he had taken to sleeping in the back seat of his silver Pontiac Trans-Am, getting respite from his marriage and work problems"

Tony forgets his duvet. The car is a Ferrari Dino 206, which broke down constantly while shooting *The Persuaders*.
Pic: Pictorial Press

SPIKE MILLIGAN:
Rarely ventured out of first gear

There are few Spike Milligan motoring anecdotes. The 'climbing into the boot of Peter Sellers' Rolls-Royce' story has also been attributed to actor Graham Stark. Milligan leapt out of a car he was driving when his soon-to-be ex-wife informed him she had spent the entire house deposit money on dancing lessons. At one stage in the 1950s he co-owned a 1920s Austin 12/4 with Peter Sellers.

"There is the occasion when Milligan leapt out a car he was actually still driving."

Milligan earned less than either Sellers or Harry Secombe for *The Goon Show* (despite writing it), and once spurned an unpaid cameo in *The Wrong Box* on the grounds that 'all of my contemporaries (i.e. Mr. Sellers) are in Rolls-Royces while I am in a Mini-Minor.' This did not stop him from appearing in TV commercials for the Mini Clubman in 1976 - the period of British Leyland history widely known as 'The Utterly Desperate Years' - nor from owning a turbo-charged model. Given that Spike would rarely venture out of first gear in his Morris Mini-Minor Super, the thought of him driving at 140 mph is not a reassuring one.

Scene from a 1970s Mini commercial
which Spike did for nothing.
Pic: Classic Cars

FORGOTTEN AVENGERS CARS:
Linda Thorson and the AC428

There were but 19 Fura-bodied AC 428 convertibles ever made and this maroon example was originally meant to be John Steed's personal transport in what turned out to be the final series of *The Avengers*. Apparently the AC was a mercifully brief attempt to modernise Steed's character, as if Patrick MacNee's alarming sideburns and the loss of Diana Rigg weren't bad enough.

In any event, Steed's use of the 428 was limited to one episode and Linda Thorson used the AC in the earlier episodes. Allegedly, Thorson couldn't drive it but so we won't be accused of sexism, let it be said that MacNee wasn't awfully fond of driving Steed's vintage Bentleys either, much of the driving being done by expert stuntman Rocky Taylor. As the series was filmed out of sequence, the AC was first seen in the Tara King/Emma Peel crossover episode but was little noticed as anyone with any degree of sensitivity was manfully blubbing at Emma's farewell. The 428 only appeared in nine episodes before being replaced by a Lotus Europa as Tara's official transport.

> "Apparently the AC was a mercifully brief attempt to modernise Steed's character."

After the slimline Elan, some felt the
brutal AC didn't cut the right dash.
Pic: Martin Buckley Archive

Thanks to everybody who made the book possible; Tony Gale at Pictorial Press for so many of the pictures, Rob Golding at Motorbooks for loving the idea and Andrew Roberts for his valuable help with research.

Martin Buckley